BICYCLING THE BACKROADS OF
NORTHWEST OREGON

Philip N. Jones

Cartoons by Dale Martin

The Mountaineers • Seattle

To my father, Captain Warren Worth Jones

THE MOUNTAINEERS: Organized 1906
"...to explore, study, preserve and enjoy
the natural beauty of the Northwest."

Published by The Mountaineers
306 Second Ave. West, Seattle, Washington 98119

Published simultaneously in Canada by Douglas & McIntyre, Ltd.
1615 Venables Street, Vancouver, British Columbia V5L 2H1

Edited by Barbara Chasan
Designed by Marge Mueller
Maps and cover photo by the author

Cover photo: Cycling near Lolo Pass (Trip #12).

Printed in the United States of America

Library of Congress Cataloging in Publication Data

Jones, Philip N.
    Bicycling the backroads of northwest Oregon.

    Includes bibliographical references and index.
    1. Bicycle touring—Oregon—Guide-books.   2. Oregon—Description and
travel—Guide-books.   I. Title.
GV1045.5.07J66   1984   917.95′043   84-6786
ISBN 0-89886-076-8

Table of Contents

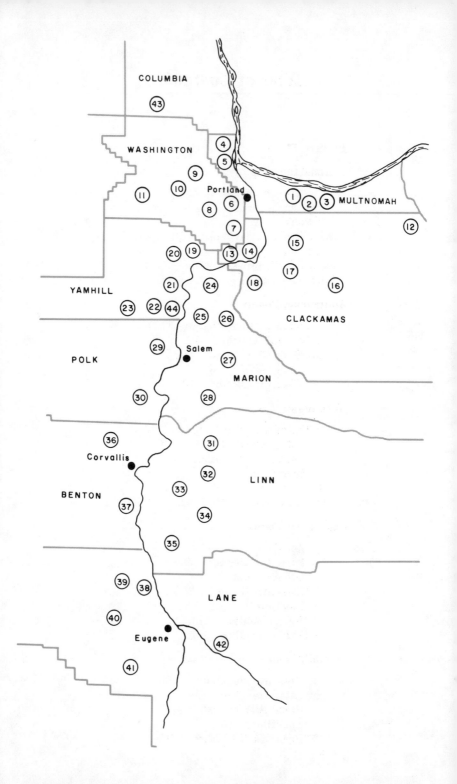

Marion County

Polk County

Linn County

Benton County

Lane County

Multi-County Rides

Indices

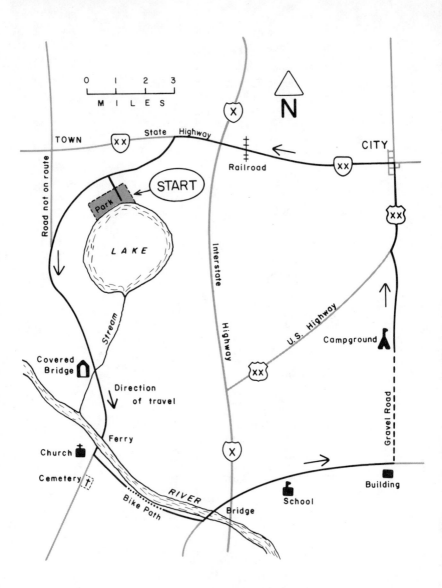

Preface

In 1972, The Mountaineers published *Bicycling the Backroads Around Puget Sound* by Erin and Bill Woods. The success of that guide, now in its fourth printing and second edition, encouraged the authors to produce a second volume, *Bicycling the Backroads of Northwest Washington* and a third, *Bicycling the Backroads of Southwest Washington.*

This fourth volume extends the tradition into Oregon. Every effort has been made to maintain the same format as the other three volumes, and to keep the same standards of quality. The author is indebted to the Woodses for the foundation they have laid, to Barclay Kruse for reviewing parts of the manuscript, and to David Puls, who helped pedal many of the routes described here. Any errors are the fault of the author, who would appreciate having them called to his attention.

Introduction

Northwestern Oregon is full of backroads, those secondary highways and county roads that provide secluded bicycling. The area also has a plentiful supply of parks, foothills, farmland, and side valleys offering superb scenery, plus small towns, ethnic settlements, and old buildings that make the riding interesting. In short, northwestern Oregon offers some of the best cycling found anywhere.

This guide is a collection of 44 bicycle trips in northwestern Oregon, principally in the Willamette Valley, from the Portland area south to the Eugene vicinity. The routes vary in length from 10 to nearly 150 miles. All but two are day trips designed to be completed in a few hours; two are long rides to be completed in a weekend of riding.

Most of the rides follow loop routes. A few are linear out-and-back routes. All avoid gravel roads and nearly all avoid main highways; the few exceptions include short sections of busy roads only when essential to connect scenic backroads. When selecting a ride, please read the trip descriptions carefully, since a few of the routes are not suitable for novice riders.

If a trip description mentions busy roads, lack of shoulders, or other safety problems, the reader will need to decide whether his or her riding skills are up to the challenge. If not, an easier ride should be chosen.

Also keep safety in mind during the course of a ride. No matter whether the ride is described as easy or safe, riders must judge for themselves whether particular conditions are safe or unsafe. If a shoulder suddenly ends, or the traffic level suddenly picks up, don't blindly pedal on, but stop to think whether the route is safe for you and your companions under the given conditions. No guidebook writer can predict future conditions, traffic levels, or cycling skills of his readers.

The Trip Descriptions

Each trip description is preceded by a capsule summary of the ride. The summaries are designed to help riders select rides that match their abilities and interests. The two most important pieces of information, the distance and the terrain, are also presented visually in elevation and distance graphs, which show the altitude profile of the route.

Don't be put off if, at first glance, a trip looks too long or too hilly. The altitude graphs greatly exaggerate the relief of the terrain covered by the routes. In addition, almost every route has shortcuts or shorter loops that can be used by less ambitious or less fit riders to reduce a ride's difficulty. Many of these alternatives are not described in the capsule summaries but are mentioned in the text of the ride descriptions or in the mileage logs. Others are readily apparent from the sketch maps.

The capsule summaries also give recommended starting times and estimates of the time required to pedal each of the routes. Neither should be considered cast in stone. The estimated times are based on how long an "average" rider might take to follow the routes, assuming a fairly slow pace and frequent stops at points of interest. A strong rider may be able to complete the routes in half the estimated times, and many of the routes would make good training rides for racers.

The recommended starting times permit riders to complete the routes by mid- to late-afternoon, based on the estimated times described above. Consider, however, the advantage of starting very early on summer mornings. Traffic will be almost nonexistent, permitting the cool morning air to be enjoyed in solitude and leaving the hot afternoon riding to late risers. Cyclists who can stand the initial agony of crawling out of bed at dawn will find their effort rewarded. In winter, another practice may be best: wait for the day to warm up a bit, then choose a short ride that will end well before the chilly late afternoon.

A map and a mileage log are provided for each trip. In theory, either one should be sufficient to guide riders along the selected route. In practice, both the map and the mileage log should be followed closely, particularly in unfamiliar territory or on routes with frequent turns or numerous intersections.

Because the mileage logs describe the trips in distances measured in tenths of a mile, an odometer is a big help when following a log. However, since the logs and maps are intended to provide enough other details to enable a rider to follow the route error-free, an odometer is not essential. If one is used, riders should not expect their mileage readings to exactly match the distances shown in the mileage logs. Bicycle odometers are not terribly exact, partly due to differences in wheel and tire sizes. Use your odometer as a rough guide.

A watch is another helpful tool to use when following a mileage log. With experience, most riders can develop a feel for how fast they are riding, and a watch can be used, with a surprising degree of accuracy, to estimate distances travelled.

The mileage logs describe each of the loop trips in either a clockwise or counter-clockwise direction. Any of the routes may be ridden in the opposite direction, although some that pass through cities and towns may require slight modification when one-way streets are encountered.

The mileage logs usually mention bike lanes or bike paths available along the routes, often with a recommendation to use them in the interest of safety. Throughout the book, a bike route on the shoulder of a road, whether designated by a painted lane or protected by small cement dividers, is referred to as a bike lane, while a paved path separate from the roadway is referred to as a bike path.

Accurate road and street names are often difficult to determine. Especially in rural areas, many roads are not signed, or they are signed with different names than those shown on local maps. Although the Oregon Department of Transportation maps purport to show the correct official name for every road in the state, those names may not be used on street signs. In this book, the road and street names used are usually the names shown on local signs. Be cautious, however. Signs can be missing, altered, or, through the efforts of local pranksters, twisted 90 degrees. Where signs conflict with available maps, or where different names appear on signs for the same road, the mileage log will show alternate names in parentheses, while the maps will show the most commonly used names. Again, both the maps and the mileage logs should be consulted to avoid losing the route.

At confusing intersections when road signs are missing or twisted, a compass may be helpful. The maps each show a scale of miles and a north arrow, and the mileage logs give compass directions at frequent intervals. When in doubt about a particular intersection, always check both the log and the map, and consult your compass if necessary.

Cyclists who find themselves turning onto a gravel road are off route; none of these rides involve gravel roads. For riders taking shortcuts or side trips away from the itineraries described here, the maps show whether nearby roads are paved or gravel. The roads of recommended alternative routes have been inspected. The pavement status of other roads is based in part on information derived from Oregon Department of Transportation maps, which are generally, but not always, accurate.

Also keep in mind that roads and intersections are constantly changing as highway departments fiddle with the landscape. Don't be surprised to find roads realigned, intersections rearranged, or new highways built. A close eye on the map and mileage log should make most changes readily apparent and wrong turns avoidable; those taken will make for interesting stories.

An attempt has also been made to describe facilities available along the routes. For those who like to buy lunch along the way, stores in rural locations are mentioned, but no attempt is made to list the hours they keep.

Public parks are mentioned if they appear along the routes or within striking distance. Nearly all have restroom facilities, if only outhouses, but many of these facilities are open only during summer months. In a few cases, budget cutbacks may have necessitated year-round closures. The presence of drinking water and camping facilities is mentioned in the mileage logs, but again, water is often disconnected and campgrounds closed in the off-season. Never count on any one source for drinking water; carry a water bottle and refill it at every opportunity.

Choosing a Bicycle

Almost any bike can be used to ride the routes described here; the bicycle needn't be fancy or expensive. A forty-pound balloon-tired bike will get you to your destination just as surely as a twenty-pound racing bike, although it may take you a bit longer. If you've got an old bike gathering dust in the garage, get it out, dust it off, make sure it is safe to ride, and start pedaling. You may eventually want to graduate to a better bike, but don't stay at home for want of a super-bike.

If you are in the market for a new bike, or looking for equipment to upgrade your old bike, here are some tips on what to look for. In general, buy the lightest bike you can. A good light bike is not really as fragile as it may appear, since the extra weight of a heavy bike is usually located in non-functional places.

The frame is a good example. Most of the stress on frame tubes comes at the ends of each tube where it is joined to the other tubes. On expensive "double-butted" frames, the wall thickness of the tubes is greatest at each end of the tubes, where strength is needed, and narrower in the mid-section of each tube, where the stress is much less. A significant amount of weight is thus saved without loss of strength.

Most frames are designed either for touring or for racing, but not for both. Touring frames are longer and more flexible than racing frames and thus produce a smoother ride. A stiff racing frame is extremely responsive but will be less comfortable on a long ride.

Bicycle frames are sized to fit different-sized bodies. The size of a frame is measured in inches or centimeters from the spindle (the axle on which the front sprockets turn) to the point where the seat post enters the frame. Most frame sizes range between 18 and 25 inches. To determine if a particular frame fits, straddle the bike, standing between the handlebars and the seat, then lift the front end of the bike. If the bike fits, you should be able to lift the front wheel an inch or two off the floor. If the frame comes up to your crotch and prevents you from lifting the front wheel, the frame you're testing is too large.

Frame size should not be confused with wheel size. While frame sizes vary, nearly all adult 10-speed bicycles use 27-inch-diameter wheels or their slightly smaller metric equivalent, 700-millimeter wheels. Some youth or inexpensive adult bikes use 26-inch wheels.

Fitting a bike to a person doesn't stop with the selection of the correct frame size. Here are some general rules to follow, but since everyone's body is different, try to get some competent advice from someone who can examine the bike and rider at the same time. The saddle height should usually be adjusted so that when the ball of one foot is on a pedal and the pedal is at its lowest position the leg will be bent slightly. The handlebars can also be raised or lowered and should usually be slightly lower than the saddle. Long- or short-armed riders might also consider changing the length of the horizontal extension of the handlebar stem, but this change requires the installation of a new stem.

After finding a bike that fits, examine the various fittings used on the bike. The rims, handlebars, pedals, cranks, and front sprockets of a heavy, inexpensive bike will all be made of steel, while these parts on a light bike will be aluminum (actually aluminum alloy). Nearly all bikes have steel alloy frames. Aluminum-frame bicycles are very rare (and very expensive). On a light bike, the only parts commonly made of steel, with the exception of the frame, will be the axles, spokes, parts of the saddle, and a few other small parts. If you can't tell the difference between aluminum and steel, carry a small magnet when shopping for a bike.

The finest, lightest components, however, can't make up for a heavy frame, nor can a light frame make up for too many steel parts. Regardless of the type of frame or fittings used, the ultimate test is the actual weight of the bicycle. A reputable dealer will not ask you to rely on weights printed in promotional brochures but will have scales on hand.

Keep in mind that the components on most bikes can be exchanged for lighter or higher quality parts. For that reason, if your budget limits your choice of bikes, buy the bike with the best frame, since the frame is the heart and soul of a bicycle. Later, a decision can be made either to buy a better bike or to upgrade some of the existing components as finances allow. When buying new components, be careful to check that the new items are compatible with your existing equipment; bike parts are not always interchangeable.

One of the most important components is the crankset, which consists of the front chainrings (sprockets), the cranks (the arms on which the pedals are mounted), and the bearings which attach the crankset to the bottom bracket of the frame. On an inexpensive bike, the cranks will be made of steel and will be attached to the spindle (bearing axle) with steel cotter pins.

Higher quality bikes use aluminum cranks attached to the spindle with bolts that screw directly into the ends of the spindle. In addition to being significantly lighter and more durable, cotterless cranks are much easier to maintain than cottered cranks.

The last few years have seen a tremendous change in bicycle wheel and tire design. Tires and rims have always been compromises between three important criteria. First, rims must be strong enough to withstand denting, and tires must be durable enough to minimize flats. Second, the tires and rims must be capable of maintaining high air pressures in order to minimize rolling resistance. Third, both rims and tires must be light in weight. Until a few years ago, riders had a Hobson's choice between two extremely different types of rims and tires. Regular "clincher" bicycle tires were durable, but they were relatively heavy and would accept only moderate air pressures. The alternative was the use of light, high-pressure racing tires, referred to as "sew-ups" or tubular tires since the edges of the tire were sewn together, completely encircling the inner tube. Sew-ups, however, are expensive and prone to flats.

The big change has been the introduction of several models of narrow clincher rims and tires that have nearly combined the best attributes of clinchers and sew-ups. While traditional clincher rims and tires were 1¼ inches wide, the new designs are one inch or 1⅛ inch wide, weigh almost as little as some sew-ups, and will accept air pressures in the neighborhood of 100 pounds per square inch. The high pressure and narrow width provide a fairly stiff ride and a small loss in traction, but the corresponding reductions in weight and rolling resistance are very appealing. The one-inch rims are also very strong, despite their light weight.

With the proliferation of new rim and tire designs, many tires are compatible only with certain rims. In general, most one-inch tires will not fit on 1¼-inch rims, nor will most 1¼-inch tires fit on one-inch rims. (In addition to requiring narrow rims, most narrow tires require narrow innertubes.) The 1⅛-inch tires, however, will generally fit on any of the rims.

Making a choice among the possible rim and tire combinations is difficult, and many riders have strong personal preferences and opinions. If you prefer the liveliest, lightest bike possible, choose one-inch rims and tires. If some luggage is to be carried or gravel roads encountered, 1⅛-inch tires could be used with the one-inch rims. For heavy loads and truly rough roads, wider rims should be employed. But most riders will find the lighter equipment to be an excellent choice for average tours on good roads. The 1⅛-inch tires are particularly useful in upgrading older bikes with 1¼-inch rims.

Special attention should be paid to the bicycle's saddle. Many bikes languish in the garages and basements of their owners due to the pain inflicted by their saddles. By shopping around, comparing different models, and soliciting recommendations from other cyclists, a reasonably comfortable saddle can be found. Traditional saddles are made solely from a piece of stiff leather and present several drawbacks. They are susceptible to damage from water (especially in the Northwest), and the less expensive models will wear out quickly. On the other hand, while uncomfortable when new, a well broken-in leather saddle is often extremely comfortable, if only to the person who broke it in. More recently, the trend has been toward plastic saddles with padded leather covers. While these models require no breaking-in period, neither do they improve in comfort over time. In the last few years, "anatomical" leather/plastic saddles with extra padding where the pelvic bones contact the saddle have become very popular, and they are considered by many to be the most comfortable saddles available.

The gears on a bike should also be chosen carefully. A multi-speed gearing system consists of a crankset with two or three chainwheels in the front and a freewheel (or cluster) with five, six, or even seven sprockets in the rear. By selecting various sizes of chainwheels and rear sprockets, gearing systems can easily be designed for particular types of riding or terrain. Yet many bicycles are delivered with poorly chosen gear combinations, and many riders fail to examine those combinations in light of their particular needs.

Even though 12-, 15-, or 18-speed bikes are becoming quite common, this discussion of gearing will use the traditional 10-speed arrangement for illustrative purposes. At best, a 10-speed bike is actually only an 8-speed bike, because the chain angle produced by using the outside chainwheel with the inside freewheel sprocket (or vice versa) is generally considered to cause excessive wear. The remaining eight gear combinations should be carefully chosen to maximize their usefulness. While racers will want those gears to be tightly grouped over a narrow range of gear ratios in order to allow for very small adjustments, most tourists will prefer a much wider range of gears, particularly in the low end range. Low gears are used for climbing hills, carrying a heavy load, or pedalling into a headwind. Higher gears are used for the downhill or when riding with a tailwind.

A particular front chainwheel used with a given rear sprocket produces a gear ratio that is usually stated (for historical reasons) as if the pedals were directly connected to a wheel of a particular diameter measured in inches. Thus, riding a bicycle with a 50-inch gear would require the same effort as riding a tricycle with a 50-inch diameter front wheel. A smaller wheel or gear is easier to pedal but requires more revolutions to move a given distance. Therefore, a 30-inch gear, which is quite small, might be a good choice for climbing steep hills, while a 100-inch gear could be used for high-speed descents. Although these inch figures can be calculated by dividing the number of front chainwheel teeth by the number of rear sprocket teeth and then multiplying by the diameter of the wheel (usually 27 inches), most riders use pre-calculated gear charts found in bicycle catalogs and manuals.

When examining gearing on a particular bike, first count the teeth on each of the chainwheels and rear sprockets, then make a list of the ten ratios that result from combining each of the two chainwheels with each of the five rear sprockets. After eliminating the two gears that are considered unusable, look closely at the remaining eight. What is the range between the highest and lowest? A low of 40 inches and a high of 100 might be considered a good compromise, but personal preferences are more important than someone else's rule of thumb. A wider range may mean undesirable large jumps between each gear but may be necessary in mountainous terrain. A smaller range will not provide the gears most riders prefer to use in hilly country but will provide the small incremental adjustments useful in flat farm country. Strong riders, who can rely on their muscles rather than their low gears to get them up hills, may prefer the close-range gearing, while beginning riders (or those planning to climb long, steep hills) will be willing to sacrifice the mid-range gears to get a very low gear.

Next, how are those eight gears spread over that range? If two of them are nearly identical (only two or three inches apart), one is being wasted. If two of them are more than 15 inches apart with no other gear in between, your ability to make small adjustments to your gearing will be limited. On a touring 10-speed, ideally none of the gears will be more than 15 or less than 5 inches from the next higher or lower gear, particularly in the middle gears, but ideals are difficult to realize without sacrificing other factors.

Another question to consider is whether both the front and rear derailleurs must be used each time the gears are shifted as the rider progresses up or down through the gear combinations. Such "double-shifting" would be fatal to a racer but is merely inconvenient to the tourist.

Of more importance to touring riders is the size of the lowest gear. If extremely steep hills are anticipated, if the rider is not in condition, or if heavy baggage will be carried, a very low gear should be sought. In such situations, a 30-inch, or even a lower gear, might be considered. Some cyclists, including this writer, believe that a 40-inch gear is adequate under most conditions, but the subject is one that will be debated as long as bicyclists ride bicycles.

If the gears on your bike are not what you want, if your fitness or riding habits change, or if you are planning to ride over unusual terrain, gearing can be changed fairly easily. Front chainwheels and rear sprockets can both be replaced, but the latter are much less expensive. Keep in mind that a gear change may also require a derailleur adjustment and an adjustment in the length of your chain.

Accessories should be added to your bicycle sparingly, since many of the available accessories add little beyond weight and clutter. Only a few should be given serious consideration. Of these, toe clips are probably the most important. While beginning riders are often reluctant to use toe clips, few riders who have given toe clips a fair chance have ever gone back to riding without them. They keep the rider's feet in place on the pedals, even when not tightly strapped, giving more control, security, and pedalling efficiency. Only when a person is first learning to ride a bike, or perhaps first learning to shift a 10-speed, could toe clips be considered a hazard.

For those who still fear toe clips, strapless "mini-clips" are available. The absence of straps gives the rider considerable freedom while maintaining a degree of control.

A good tire pump should also be mounted on the bike. Choose your pump carefully, since some models are not capable of the high pressures required by modern tires and others will reach high pressures only when powered by a professional weight lifter. Also make sure that the pump fits the valves of your bike: Schrader valves are the same type used on automobile tires, while Presta valves are narrower.

In the Northwest, fenders will greatly extend the bicycling season. Most models of fenders add very little in weight but add a great deal in comfort when rain strikes.

Many riders extoll the safety virtues of rear-view mirrors. Models are available that mount on the bike, on the helmet, or even mount on eyeglasses.

A handlebar bag is very useful on day trips for carrying food, extra clothes, maps, and a tool kit. Training racers usually carry the bare necessities in their pockets or tied under their saddles, but most touring riders will want to carry a bit more.

Water is best carried in a plastic pint bottle carried in a metal cage mounted on the bike frame. The bottles and cages are inexpensive and permit drinking while en route. Aluminum cages are rustproof and lighter than steel models.

Clothing

Like any outdoor activity, bicycling requires proper clothing. In western Oregon, the usual problem is keeping warm and dry. Occasionally the problem is keeping cool. Just as a top-line bicycle is not essential, so state-of-the-art clothing may be desirable, but its absence is hardly reason to sit home. In most cases, specialized bicycling clothes are not necessary, and an assortment of items from the back of the closet will do nicely.

Shoes are a good example. In general, cyclists have three choices. The most expensive, and the choice of all racers and many tourists, are the light leather or synthetic cycling shoes with very stiff soles and metal or plastic cleats. The cleats fit over the rear plates of the pedal cages and, when combined with toe clips, produce a very positive attachment to the pedal. The stiff soles are particularly important on long rides, when softer soles would eventually permit the feet to feel the pedal cages.

On the other end of the spectrum, many recreational riders use conventional running shoes, which generally work fairly well if the chosen model has a thick sole and a narrow heel. The flared heel found on some running shoes will catch on the crank arm with each pedal revolution.

Other shoes have recently been introduced that fall somewhere between these two extremes. Specially designed for bike touring, they combine the appearance and walking comfort of running shoes with soles sufficiently stiff to ensure comfortable long-distance pedalling. These touring shoes do not employ cleats, but some models have grooved soles that are designed to grip the pedal cage.

Due to their light weight, most bike shoes are not suitable for winter use.

Although insulated winter bicycling shoes are available, most riders improvise for the occasional cold-weather ride. Lightweight hiking shoes may be worn, or insulated booties are available that fit over cycling shoes.

Shorts and pants are probably the most important items of clothing. Long hours on the saddle require that every effort be made to keep comfortable. Taking a tip from racers, many serious touring riders use knitted wool or synthetic shorts lined with a chamois seat. In cold weather, knitted leg warmers can be attached to the shorts. Many recreational riders make do with a variety of other types of shorts, and in cool weather they carry either long underwear, cycling tights, or a pair of long pants. One cold-weather option is to wear wool knickers. A fine pair of light knickers can be made out of an old pair of wool dress slacks, particularly if the waist is let out an inch or two. Knickers, long pants, or leg warmers also help prevent abrasions in the event of a fall.

Shirts, or jerseys as cyclists prefer to call them, are not as crucial as shorts but are still important for comfort. As with shorts, racers and many serious tourists opt for specially designed wool or synthetic knit jerseys with pockets on the back for food, etc. (Pockets on the front sag during a ride.) Less specialized, but equally effective, are light turtlenecks. In summer, cotton (preferably a light color) should be favored. T-shirts are commonly-worn, but a long-sleeved shirt protects the rider from sunburn.

In summer, a white cotton bicycling cap keeps the head cool, while in winter a wool stocking cap (or even a balaclava) keeps the head warm. In any season, however, the safety of a helmet makes it the clear choice for headgear. Some models will adjust in size to permit the rider to wear a light stocking cap in cold weather.

In wet weather, a complete waterproof suit is ideal, particularly if made of one of the new breathable waterproof fabrics such as Gore-tex or Klimate. If the rain is not particularly cold, wool will usually be sufficient to keep the rider fairly comfortable. But in any kind of weather, an extra windbreaker or sweater should be carried, just in case.

Bicycle gloves provide added comfort on a long ride, and they also protect the hands in the event of a crash. Most cycling gloves have padded palms but are fingerless.

Maintenance and Tools

One of the joys of relying on a bicycle for transportation is the knowledge that it is a simple machine that can be maintained and repaired by anyone, even those with minimal mechanical inclination or ability. The riders who leave the repair work to someone else are missing a satisfying aspect of bicycling, in addition to placing themselves at the mercy of circumstances if their bike breaks down far from a repair shop.

Even if you don't enjoy working on your bike and would rather pay someone else to do it, learning to maintain and repair your bike does more than prevent your having to hitchhike back to town; it teaches you to spot dangerous conditions like frayed brake cables, worn tires, and loose fenders. Eventually you will come to know your bike like an old friend. Its slightest malady will be made immediately apparent by such subtle symptoms as a funny clicking noise, a soft brake lever, or an unresponsive derailleur.

You can't expect to jump right in and start fixing everything and anything on your bike right away, but understanding the basics won't take very long. Start out with a good bike repair book. The author's (and probably everybody else's) personal favorite is *Anybody's Bike Book* by Tom Cuthbertson, published by Ten Speed Press. It doesn't cover everything, but it comes pretty close, and it does it with great style. The next step is to cultivate a relationship with a bike addict or a repair person at your local shop who can help out with those tricky one-of-a-kind problems. A good bike shop will cheerfully answer questions and help find those little parts that never seem to be available. Bike repair classes are also available from bike shops, park departments, or evening college programs.

When working on your bike, specialized tools are generally not needed, and the few essential ones are not expensive. You will, however, want to buy a few light tools to carry when touring. An ultra-light tool kit might include the following:

1. Two or three tire irons, preferably of aluminum or plastic rather than steel, for prying clincher tires off rims.
2. A patch kit for repairing punctured tubes. Many riders don't bother to fix punctures on the road but simply install a new tube. On long rides, carry both a patch kit and a new tube.
3. An Allen wrench or two, depending on the bike.
4. A small screwdriver.
5. Twenty-five cents. The ten-cent phone call is long gone.

A lengthy ride would justify carrying a heavier tool kit, which might include the above items plus some of the following:

6. A small (six-inch) adjustable wrench, such as a Crescent wrench, or a few socket wrenches.
7. An extra brake cable.
8. A spoke wrench.
9. Extra spokes. These can be carried taped to the frame or even bent and stuffed inside the handlebars.
10. A crank remover.
11. A freewheel remover.
12. A chain tool.

This list could go on endlessly, limited only by the countless mechanical failures one can imagine occurring on a ride, but the temptation to carry an extensive tool kit should be resisted.

Safe Riding

Bicycle riding is a generally safe activity, but riders must be cautious of some potential dangers. The single most significant danger is the careless motorist. Many motorists are in the habit of watching out for only those vehicles that are as large as the ones they drive. To them, anything on the road smaller than another car is either not seen or, even worse, seen but disregarded.

Bicyclists must constantly battle this danger. The battle is waged using three tactics. First, cyclists must make themselves seen. Second, cyclists must ride defensively. Third, cyclists must ride responsibly.

Cyclists should try to make themselves visible at all times by wearing bright clothing, bright helmets, reflective material, or anything else that a motorist will see easily and quickly. In addition, bicyclists should try to ride a straight line, rather than constantly pulling in and out of traffic; motorists understandably have a difficult time keeping track of a bike that is continually disappearing and reappearing.

Defensive riding requires a bit more explanation. It is simply the art of avoiding situations where cyclists have no control over their own safety. On a broad, busy highway, defensive riding means staying on the shoulder out of the flow of traffic. At intersections, defensive riding means not pulling out in front of a moving car, even if the cyclist has the right of way.

In some cases, defensive riding must necessarily evolve into "offensive" riding. For example, when heavy traffic is present on narrow roads, safety may require the cyclist to ride in the center of the lane. This technique of "taking the lane" is an acceptable one if it is necessary to force traffic to recognize the cyclist's presence. By taking the lane on a narrow road, a cyclist forces cars to treat the bicycle as a vehicle that must be passed using the opposite lane, just as any other vehicle would be passed. Obviously, taking the lane on a high-speed highway is suicide, but in situations where a bicyclist is sure to be seen and recognized by motorists, taking the lane is preferable to being sideswiped on a narrow shoulder or being forced to ride inches away from parked cars or a soft gravel shoulder. It is a particularly useful technique on city streets where bikes can keep up with the flow of traffic.

The third tactic, responsible riding, may not produce results as immediate as the first two procedures, but it is equally important. If we, as bicyclists, insist that motorists respect our right to use the roadway, we must first show similar respect for motorists. If we are to shed the image of children playing in the streets, we must ride as though we were adults pursuing a serious form of transportation and recreation. In other words, bicyclists must act lawfully, predictably, and courteously. Turns must be signaled, stop signs and traffic lights obeyed, and a single file formed when being overtaken by cars. The same courtesy we demand from motorists must be shown them in return.

Partly as the result of amendments made in 1983, Oregon laws now give

bicyclists substantial rights on the roadways of the state. The statutes specifically state that bicycles are now considered vehicles, and as such they have all of the rights and responsibilities of motor vehicles. Prior to 1983, the statutes had also stipulated that bicycles must be operated as close to the right shoulder of the road "as is practicable." The statutes now provide that bicyclists may use any portion of the lane if they can keep up with the flow of traffic and may also take the lane in faster traffic if the lane is too narrow to allow cars to pass safely. Thus, "offensive" riding is legal when necessary in the interest of safety; otherwise, cyclists must either keep up with traffic or keep to the right. On one-way streets, cyclists may keep either to the right or the left.

The statutes also require courteous and responsible riding. All traffic signals must be obeyed, all turns must be signaled, and riding two abreast is permitted only when the normal flow of traffic is not impeded. One innovation stipulates that bicyclists may signal for a right turn by simply extending their right arms horizontally, rather than extending their left arms upward.

The statutes also address the use of bike paths. Many cyclists dislike bike paths, pointing out that the paths are often narrow, twisting, blocked by pedestrians, and littered with leaves, broken glass, and gravel. In answer to these concerns, the law provides that when a bike path is available adjacent to a roadway, cyclists are free to choose between the roadway and the path. The statutes specify that the use of a bike path can be mandated only if the local government has held a public hearing and determined that the particular bike path is suitable for reasonable rates of speed.

In addition to road tactics, safe riding requires safe equipment. Inspect your bike frequently; get to know it well. Know when the brakes need adjustment; know when wheels are out of true; know when the headset is loose or when tires are worn. And remember what happens when one of those pieces of equipment fails. Bombing down steep hills is great fun, but a blowout at 40 miles per hour is a serious affair.

One piece of safety equipment evokes more strong opinions than any other. Riders who don't wear helmets claim they are hot and impair hearing. Riders who do wear helmets have a simple response: helmets save lives. Even low-speed accidents can result in serious or fatal head injuries.

One element of safe riding is practiced off the bike. Safe riding requires that roads and other public facilities be designed for safe use by bicycles. With public funds in short supply and legislatures and city councils dealing with countless other issues, bicyclists must vocalize their concerns loudly. The results can be dramatic; the 1983 amendments to the motor vehicle code were largely the work of bike activists. Many bicycle clubs have become politically active. Perhaps the most notable example is a Portland organization, Tri-County Bicyclists United, P.O. Box 14075, Portland OR 97214, which was formed for the express purpose of improving bicycling conditions. They, and other organizations like them, deserve your support and active participation.

Maps for Touring

The ideal bicycling map should be small enough to be conveniently carried and used on the road but sufficiently detailed to show every single road and intersection. It should accurately name all roads, and indicate which are paved and which are not. It should include topographic contour lines, along with cultural facilities such as small towns and public parks. It should be completely up to date and printed in a readable fashion.

Such maps do not exist. Perhaps unavoidably, available maps have all compromised one or more of the above qualities. The maps included in this guide also display compromises and shortcomings, but the author hopes they will guide the reader on the trips with a minimum danger of wrong turns.

Many readers will want to obtain other maps, to connect two or more of the loops described here, or to plot their own trips in the Willamette Valley or elsewhere. A discussion of available maps may help the reader find a map that will satisfy those needs.

In general, road maps of the type gas stations once gave away are inadequate for bicycle touring. The state maps are simply not sufficiently detailed to show backroads, and the city maps are limited to large cities and their immediate suburbs. A few city maps, however, do include small regional inserts that can be helpful.

U.S. Geological Survey topographic maps are available in several scales, but most of the available scales are either too large, meaning the area covered is so small that several sheets must be carried, or are too small, so that roads are not shown in sufficient detail. For example, the scale on the USGS 1:250,000 series maps is too small, and the scale on their 1:24,000 series (7.5 minute) maps is too large. Their 1:62,500 series (15 minute) is a good compromise in terms of both size and detail, but few, if any, of the maps in that series have been updated recently, and thus roads and other cultural features are often not shown accurately. (Eventually, the 15-minute series will be phased out entirely.) Moreover, none of the topographic maps shows whether particular backroads are paved.

A new series of 1:100,000 60-minute metric topographic maps is in the process of being produced by the USGS in a 31- by 22-inch size. The scale is excellent for bike touring purposes, cultural features are up-to-date, and the maps are easy to carry because they come folded like gas station maps. The only drawbacks are a relatively high price and a lack of pavement status of backroads.

The most reliable, although not always perfectly accurate, information about pavement status is available from maps published by state highway departments in cooperation with the Federal Highway Administration. These inexpensive maps are published on a county-by-county basis; maps of some of the larger counties cover more than one sheet of paper. Of the several scales published, three should be of interest to bike tourists.

The General Highway Series, although quite large (36 by 42 inches), shows every public road with a usually accurate indication of whether each is paved, but for some reason it doesn't give road names. A separate Road Index Series is published in the same scale, but the maps do not indicate pavement status. Given a choice between these two series, riders who wish to avoid gravel roads will prefer the General Highway Series and will get along without road names. As the highway department revises its maps, the need to make this choice will slowly disappear. The General Highway Series maps that have been revised recently now show most road names, and the revised Road Index Series maps now show pavement status. In a few years, when maps for all 36 counties will have been revised, either of the two series will suffice.

A third series, probably the most useful to bicyclists, is the General Highway Series published in a smaller size (17.5 by 20 inches). This "half-size" series is not only less expensive and easier to carry than the larger series, it is printed in color and thus is quite easy to read. An atlas of black-and-white 8.5- by 11-inch "quarter-size" maps is also available for a few dollars; its maps are particularly useful for photocopying and carrying on the road.

In addition to the drawback of not including road names and pavement status on the same map, all of these highway department maps lack detail in cities and towns. Not to fear, however, for a fifth series of maps of cities and a sixth series of maps of towns are available, along with a seventh series of aerial photos of most urban areas. Or, for the ultimate in map trivia, straight-line maps of state highways are available that show every intersection, railroad crossing, bridge, and culvert, all measured to within one hundredth of a mile.

If you're interested in these and other maps, you should consider building an addition on your house in which to store them all and then write for a free map index and ordering information from the Oregon Department of Transportation, Map Distribution Unit, Room 17, Transportation Building, Salem, Oregon 97310. For maps in Washington, write the Washington Department of Transportation, Public Transportation and Planning, Highway Administration Building, Olympia, Washington 98504.

County maps are also available commercially under several brand names. While they are not as inexpensive as the highway department maps described above, they do show most roads and road names on the same map, together with some detail in cities and towns. Most of the commercial maps are quite large, however, and thus difficult to use on the road. On some, the pavement status is either not shown or does not appear to be as accurate as the state maps; others appear to be substantially reprinted from the state maps. Shop around to find a brand that combines the features you need.

For bicycling within cities, city street maps are generally adequate. If gas station maps are not available, the city maps published by the state are excellent. In addition, the larger cities in the Willamette Valley have now published street maps designed expressly for bicyclists. The *Portland Bicycle Map*, available from the Bicycle and Pedestrian Program, Room 834, 1120 S.W. Fifth Avenue, Portland, Oregon 97204, uses a color coding system to classify every street in the city as to its suitability for biking. The *Salem Bicycle Map* uses the same system. It is available from the Salem Public Works Department, 555 Liberty Street, Salem, Oregon 97301. The *Eugene Bicycle Map*, available from the Eugene Bicycle Committee, 858 Pearl Street, Eugene, Oregon 97401, uses a similar system, although not all streets are coded. A Corvallis bike route map, *Corvallis Area Bikeways*, is available from the Corvallis Engineering Department, P.O. Box 1083, Corvallis, Oregon 97339. With the exception of the Corvallis map, each city charges a small fee for its bike map, which can also be purchased at local bike shops.

The metropolitan area around Portland is covered by an excellent bike map similar to the successful Portland Bicycle Map. Entitled *Getting There By Bike*, it is available for a small charge from the Metropolitan Service District, 527 S.W. Hall Street, Portland, Oregon 97201, or from local bike shops.

For biking outside of cities, the state of Oregon has published several maps and pamphlets. One, *Oregon Bike Routes*, shows several cross-state routes. The north-south coastal route is also shown in greater detail in a brochure entitled "Oregon Coast Bike Route." Another brochure, "Oregon Bikeways," lists 74 short bike lanes and bike paths. A fourth brochure, "Willamette River Cycling Guide," describes nearly 20 rides along the Willamette River, including an excellent route between Portland and

Eugene. All of the above brochures are available free of charge at many bike shops or by writing to the Department of Transportation, Salem, Oregon 97310.

The Astoria-to-Idaho route described in the "Oregon Bike Routes" pamphlet was established in 1976 by Bikecentennial. That organization has published detailed maps and guides to the route and to several other cross-country routes. A catalog of maps and books is available from Bikecentennial, P.O. Box 8308, Missoula, Montana 59807.

For riders heading north into Washington, the Cascade Bicycle Club of Seattle has published a map that shows a Portland-to-Seattle route that avoids most main highways. The map, which was developed for the popular Seattle-to-Portland ride held each year in June, is available from the Cascade Bicycle Club, P.O. Box 12774, Seattle, Washington 98111, or from Bikecentennial.

Further Reading

The foregoing introduction to bicycle touring is all too brief. For the reader looking for more information, here are some suggested sources.

At least two other guides to bicycling in western Oregon have been published in recent years. In 1973, Touchstone Press issued *55 Oregon Bicycle Trips* by Nick and Elske Jankowski, which describes day trips in the Willamette Valley and on the northern Oregon coast. A year earlier, two Eugene cyclists, Ernie Drapela and Kevin Pratt, published *30 Bike Rides in Lane County*. Both volumes are now out of print but often can be found in public libraries and used book stores.

In 1982, the Bicycle Commuter Service published *Portland by Bicycle*, an excellent small guide to 16 day trips in Portland.

Good advice on techniques for day trips can be found in *Bike Tripping* by Tom Cuthbertson (Ten Speed Press, 1972). For comprehensive advice on nearly every aspect of bicycle touring, with emphasis on longer rides, try *Bike Touring: The Sierra Club Guide to Outings on Wheels,* by Raymond Bridge (Sierra Club, 1979).

For exploring the nooks and crannies of the Willamette Valley (and elsewhere in Oregon), few volumes contain the wealth of information found in *Oregon for the Curious* by Ralph Friedman (Caxton Printers, 1974) and *Oregon Geographic Names* by Lewis A. McArthur (Oregon Historical Society, 1982).

Riders heading north into Washington will want to consult Erin and Bill Woods' *Bicycling the Backroads* books (The Mountaineers), which cover southwest Washington, the Puget Sound area, and northwest Washington.

"Schwinns at 6 o'clock!"

1 COLUMBIA RIVER HIGHWAY

Starting Point: Lewis and Clark State Park, near Troutdale, just south of I-84 exit 18.
Distance: up to 49.8 miles.
Terrain: Hilly.
Total Cumulative Elevation Gain: 1900 feet.
Recommended Time of Year: Any season, except when freezing conditions exist in the Columbia River Gorge.
Recommended Starting Time: 9:00 A.M.
Allow: 6 hours.

Points of Interest
Columbia River Gorge
Eight state parks
Vista House at Crown Point
Columbia River Highway bridges
Numerous waterfalls

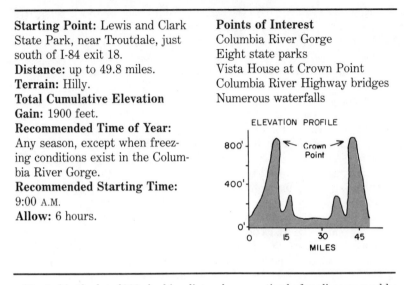

Started in the late 1800s by bicyclists who were tired of cycling on muddy roads, the "Good Roads" movement gained strength in the early 1900s when automobiles became available to the masses. In the Northwest the movement was championed by railroad attorney Sam Hill, who had a vision of a beautiful highway built through the Columbia River Gorge, a road to be constructed in complete harmony with its surroundings.

Construction began in 1913 with the political and financial assistance of lumberman Simon Benson and a newly formed state highway commission. Lumberman John Yeon helped by serving as Multnomah County Roadmaster for two years without pay, and Samuel Lancaster, back from a tour of roads in the Alps with Sam Hill, was hired as supervising engineer.

When the highway opened in 1915, it was acclaimed as both an engineering marvel and an aesthetic masterpiece. Sensitive design by Lancaster, together with the painstaking skills of immigrant stonemasons, created a highway to be respected, not as a primary transportation route, but as a special roadway to be savored at a slow pace, mindful of the inspired craftsmanship that created it. Despite the awesome terrain of the Gorge, nowhere did the slope of the road exceed 5 percent, nor were any of the curves on less than a one-hundred-foot radius. The careful placement of the roadbed, miles and miles of hand-built stone railings, dozens of beautiful bridges (of which no two were identical), and several basalt tunnels were the principal features that brought widespread acclaim to the highway.

Following the second world war, however, the public wanted more than "good roads." They wanted interstate freeways, and the picturesque

Columbia River Highway grew obsolete. Construction of what is now Interstate 84 began in 1948 and would eventually destroy much of Lancaster's work.

Today, the western half of the highway from Troutdale to Warrendale remains intact, as does the easternmost section from Mosier to The Dalles. In between, from Warrendale to Mosier, the old highway has been badly segmented by the freeway construction. Many segments have been destroyed, and others have been abandoned, neglected, or, at best, poorly preserved.

The ride described below covers the intact western half of the highway, starting near Troutdale, slowly climbing up over Crown Point, then descending to near water level, to pass at the feet of many of the Gorge's spectacular waterfalls. Although the entire western section of 24.9 miles is described as an out-and-back trip of 49.8 miles, it can be shortened by a U-turn at any point, or the ride can be started at any of the numerous parks or waterfalls along the highway. For example, the climb over Crown Point can be avoided by starting at Latourell Falls, just east of Crown Point. Riders planning to travel more than a few miles will want to pack a lunch to enjoy at one of the parks or waterfalls.

One caution: the Columbia River Highway was designed for Model Ts. It is narrow, twisting, and, on sunny days, populated by tourists paying more attention to the scenery than to the road. Ride carefully.

MILEAGE LOG

0.0 Lewis and Clark State Park (day use only; water available). Leave the parking lot and turn left. Follow this road past the Troutdale bridge at mile 0.3, where it joins the **Columbia River Highway**. Pass the Stark Street bridge at mile 2.9. The entrance to Dabney State Park (day use only; water available) is on the right at mile 3.3.

4.6 Springdale. Bear right, following the signs to Crown Point.

4.8 Bear left at the intersection with Hurlburt Road.

6.3 Corbett.

8.8 Portland Women's Forum State Park (day use only; water available). Probably the most famous view of the Columbia River Gorge is available from this park located at Chanticleer Point.

9.2 Intersection with Larch Mountain Road. Bear left.

10.0 Crown Point State Park, consisting of the Vista House, conceived by Lancaster as an observatory from which the Columbia Gorge "could be viewed in silent communion with the infinite." Used until recently as a souvenir center, the Vista House is now serving as an interpretive center. The highway curves around the front of Vista House, then drops (at a 5-percent rate, of course) through a series of Lancaster's graceful one-hundred-foot curves.

12.4 Latourell Falls day-use area, part of Guy Talbot State Park (day use only; water available). Walk your bike up a short path for a full view of the falls. Also note the craftsmanship of the highway bridge over

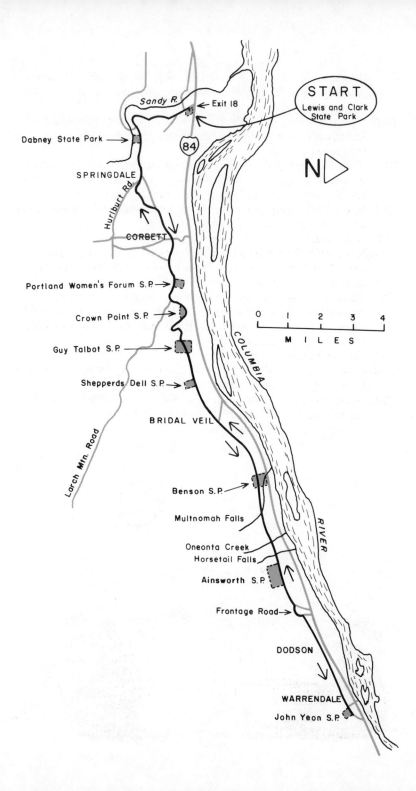

START
Lewis and Clark
State Park

Sandy R. ← Exit 18

84

Dabney State Park →

SPRINGDALE

Hurlburt Rd.

CORBETT

Portland Women's Forum S.P. →

Crown Point S.P. →

Guy Talbot S.P. →

Shepperds Dell S.P. →

BRIDAL VEIL

COLUMBIA

N ▷

0   1   2   3   4
M I L E S

Larch Mtn. Road

Benson S.P. →

Multnomah Falls

Oneonta Creek

Horsetail Falls

Ainsworth S.P.

RIVER

Frontage Road →

DODSON

WARRENDALE

John Yeon S.P.

Latourell Creek. It is probably the only braced spandrel, concrete, arched bridge in the state, and one of the first built in the United States.

13.7 Shepperds Dell State Park (day use only; water not available). A short path at the east end of the bridge gives excellent views of the bridge and Shepperds Dell Falls.

14.7 Bridal Veil Bridge. This small bridge is supported by its solid railings, rather than supported from below, to allow clearance for the three log flumes and the small dam which once lay beneath it.

15.3 Bridal Veil. Continue east on the **Columbia River Highway**, rather than turning left to the freeway.

17.9 Wahkeena Falls, part of Benson State Park.

18.5 Multnomah Falls, the highest in Oregon at a combined height of 620 feet (store; drinking water). On both sides of the falls, the highway traverses steep ground on concrete viaducts.

20.8 Oneonta Creek. The present highway bridge was built in 1948 to replace the original 1914 bridge, which is now used as a wayside. Note the evidence of the tunnel to the east, which was closed when the new bridge was built.

21.1 Horsetail Falls.

21.6 Ainsworth State Park picnic area. An overnight camping area is located at mile 22.1 (drinking water available).

22.4 Intersection with I-84. Turn right, following the signs toward I-84 eastbound. A short section of the old highway was destroyed by the construction of this interchange.

22.7 Turn right on **Frontage Road**. At mile 22.8, Frontage Road rejoins the old alignment of the **Columbia River Highway**.

23.1 Dodson. The large barn on the south side of the road was built circa 1870. Above it sits a basalt formation known as Saint Peters Dome.

24.0 Warrendale.

24.9 John Yeon State Park (day use only; no drinking water). East of this point, the old highway was destroyed by the construction of I-84. This is the eastern end of the ride described here. Make a U-turn and proceed west, retracing the route back to Lewis and Clark State Park.

49.8 Lewis and Clark State Park. End of ride.

Multnomah County

2 LARCH MOUNTAIN

Starting Point: Portland Women's Forum State Park (Chanticleer Point), one mile west of Crown Point on the Columbia River Highway (the scenic highway).
Distance: 30.2 miles.
Terrain: Very hilly.
Total Cumulative Elevation Gain: 3220 feet.
Recommended Time of Year: Any season except winter.
Recommended Starting Time: Before 11:00 A.M.
Allow: 4 hours.

Points of Interest
Chanticleer Point
Summit of Larch Mountain

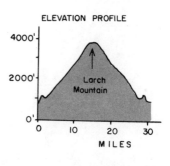

The steep basalt cliffs of the Columbia River Gorge were created as the river cut its course downward through the rising Cascade Range. Due to the steep terrain, fairly high peaks now stand short distances from the near sea-level Columbia. Larch Mountain is an excellent example: although it is more than four thousand feet high, it lies only three and a half miles from the river.

This ride follows a well-paved road to within a few feet of the summit of Larch Mountain, a former volcano. The route starts at Portland Women's Forum State Park, a prominent viewpoint 840 feet above the river. Even so, the ride presents a three-thousand-foot climb, averaging more than a

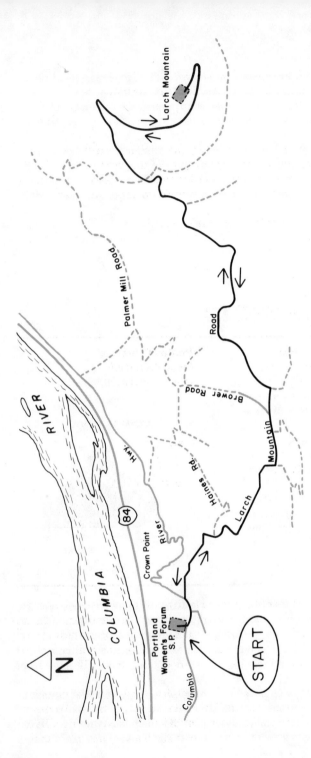

N

COLUMBIA RIVER

RIVER

84 Hwy

Crown Point

River

Columbia

Portland Women's Forum S.P.

START

Palmer Mill Road

Brower Road

Haines Rd.

Larch Mountain

Road

Larch Mountain

MILES
0   1   2

hundred feet of elevation gain each mile. While the road is never truly steep, it climbs the mountain at a steady rate, with very few level stretches.

The ride can also be started at Lewis and Clark State Park near Troutdale, for a round trip of 47.8 miles and a cumulative elevation gain of 4050 feet. (The ride from Lewis and Clark State Park to Portland Women's Forum State Park is described as the first 8.8 miles of Trip #1.)

The road ends at a Forest Service picnic ground near the summit of the mountain. For the best views of Mount Hood, your bike can be walked up a short trail (and carried up a few steps) to Sherrard Point, just north of the true summit.

The descent from the summit of Larch Mountain will be a fast one, perhaps taking less than half an hour. Check your brakes before you start, and be careful of the many curves.

Larch Mountain was apparently named for the larch, a tree unusual for the fact that its foliage consists of needles, like many evergreens, yet the larch is deciduous and thus loses its needles in the fall. In late September of each year, larches turn a beautiful yellow hue as their needles begin to drop. That's no reason to ride up Larch Mountain in September, however, since not a single larch tree has been found on Larch Mountain. In Oregon, larches grow only on the east side of the Cascades.

Due to the location and elevation of Larch Mountain, the weather will play an important role in planning this ride. The Columbia River Gorge is noted for terrible weather and for rapid changes in weather. Consult a current forecast, and if the weather turns for the worse during your ride consider making a quick descent. This advice is particularly important during periods of cold weather, when snow and freezing rain are always possibilities in the Gorge.

When snow does come to the Gorge, Larch Mountain Road generally cannot be ridden for some time thereafter, since the road is usually not plowed beyond mile 7.0. If in doubt about weather or snow conditions, call the Forest Service's Columbia Gorge Ranger Station at (503) 695-2276.

MILEAGE LOG

0.0 Portland Women's Forum State Park. Park at Chanticleer Point, the lower (northern) end of the park, then ride south, out of the park, toward the Columbia River Highway.

0.1 Turn left on the **Columbia River Highway**.

0.5 Bear right on **Larch Mountain Road**. Follow Larch Mountain Road all the way to the picnic ground near the summit of Larch Mountain.

15.1 Larch Mountain parking lot and picnic ground. A quarter-mile trail leads to a viewpoint. After lunch or a rest, retrace the route back down to your car.

29.7 Turn left on **Columbia River Highway**.

30.1 Turn right into Portland Women's Forum State Park.

30.2 Chanticleer Point. End of ride.

3 SANDY RIVER GORGE

Starting Point: Lewis and Clark State Park, near Troutdale, just south of I-84 exit 18.
Distance: 39.4 miles.
Terrain: Very hilly.
Total Cumulative Elevation Gain: 2700 feet.
Recommended Time of Year: Any season, except during possible snowy conditions.
Recommended Starting Time: 10:00 A.M.
Allow: 5 hours.

Points of Interest
Lewis and Clark State Park
Dabney State Park
Sandy River Gorge
Bull Run Gorge
Roslyn Lake

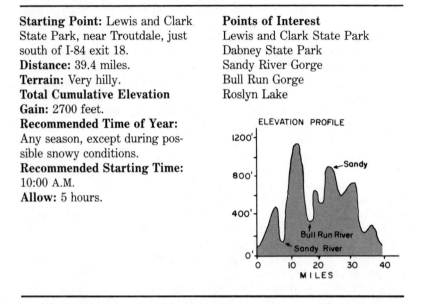

ELEVATION PROFILE

The Sandy River and its tributary, the Bull Run, have cut deep gorges into the foothills west of Mount Hood. This ride descends into the Sandy gorge three times and the Bull Run once, in each case making a steep climb back out again. Since the three climbs each involve elevation gains of several hundred feet, and one has a gain of more than a thousand feet, this is not a ride for flatlanders, although the trip traverses several flat plateaus between each gorge. The plateaus, by the way, offer rewarding views of Mount Hood and the surrounding foothills.

The several descents are not only long and steep; some are on narrow, fairly rough roads. Make certain your bike is in good condition, paying particular attention to its brakes and tires.

The ride visits or passes within striking distance of at least five parks. Lewis and Clark and Dabney state parks are located along the lower Sandy River, while Oxbow and Dodge county parks are further up the Sandy River Gorge. Roslyn Lake Park, operated by the public utility company that created the man-made lake, lies on a plateau between the Sandy and Bull Run gorges.

The trip begins at Lewis and Clark State Park near the mouth of the Sandy, then slowly climbs past Dabney State Park to Springdale, where the route turns south to make a sudden and very steep drop, returning to the Sandy River. At its lowest point, the road skirts the river near Oxbow Park, then climbs steeply out of the gorge to the flat farmland surrounding

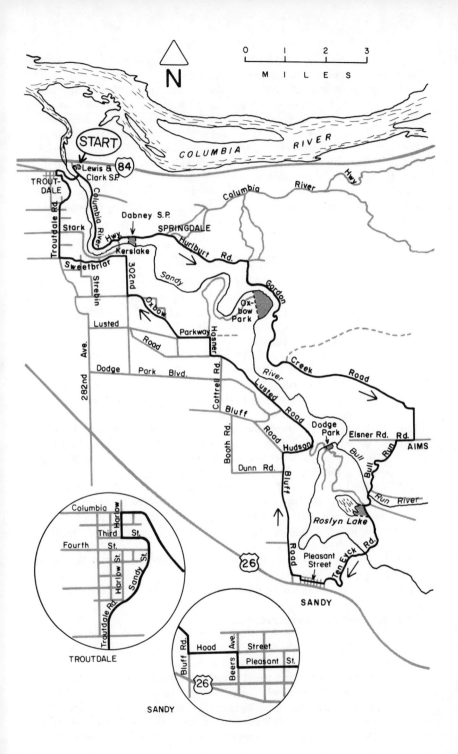

START

84

Lewis & Clark S.P.

TROUT-
DALE

Columbia River Hwy

Troutdale Rd.

Stark

Sweetbriar

Strebin

282nd Ave.

Dabney S.P.

Kerslake

SPRINGDALE

Hurlburt Rd.

Columbia River

Hwy

Sandy

302nd

Oxbow

Lusted

Parkway

Hogan

Oxbow Park

Gordon

Road

Dodge Park Blvd.

Cottrell Rd.

Bluff Road

Booth Rd.

Dunn Rd.

Lusted Road

River

Creek

Road

Dodge Park

Hudson

Elsner Rd.

Bull Run Rd.

AIMS

Bull Run River

Bluff

Road

Roslyn Lake

Ten Eyck Rd.

26

Pleasant Street

SANDY

COLUMBIA RIVER

Columbia River

Hwy

N

0   1   2   3
M I L E S

TROUTDALE

Columbia
Third St.
Harlow St.
Fourth St.
Harlow St.
Sandy St.
Troutdale Rd.

SANDY

Bluff Rd.
Hood
Beers Ave.
Street
Pleasant St.
26

35

the nearly nonexistent community of Aims.

The flat riding is short-lived, since the road makes another sudden and steep drop, this time to the Bull Run River, then immediately climbs 350 feet to Roslyn Lake. After another short flat section, the route drops back into the Sandy River Gorge, then climbs to the town of Sandy and the farmland north of the town. A final drop into and out of the gorge (which can be avoided by a level shortcut) is followed by a pleasant ride to Troutdale through east Multnomah County farmland.

For some reason, the Sandy River area seems afflicted with very poor signing. Many road signs are missing or inaccurate. If any intersections seem confusing, study the map and mileage log carefully.

MILEAGE LOG

0.0 Lewis and Clark State Park. Leave the parking lot and turn left. Follow this road past the Troutdale bridge at mile 0.3 where it joins the **Columbia River Highway**. Pass the Stark Street bridge at 2.9 miles. The entrance to Dabney State Park (day use only; water available) is on the right at 3.3 miles.

4.6 Springdale. Bear right, following the sign to Crown Point.

4.8 Bear right on **Hurlburt Road**.

6.8 Turn right on **Gordon Creek Road**. At mile 7.3, the road makes a sudden and steep decline into the Sandy River Gorge. Gordon Creek Road eventually becomes **Bull Run Road**.

15.0 Aims. At the T-intersection, turn right, following Bull Run Road.

15.5 At an intersection with Elsner Road, turn left, following Bull Run Road as it begins another steep descent. At mile 17.5, cross a bridge over the Bull Run River, then begin a steep climb.

18.1 Roslyn Lake. Turn left on **Ten Eyck Road** (unmarked). (To the right, a dike along the lake offers a place to lunch or rest.) At mile 18.7 is the entrance to Roslyn Lake Park (Thomas Road). Continue on Ten Eyck Road as it descends to the Sandy River at mile 19.8 and then climbs to the town of Sandy.

21.7 Sandy. Turn right on **Pleasant Street**, which is one block before an intersection with U.S. 26.

22.3 At a T-intersection with **Beers Avenue**, turn right and ride one block north.

22.4 Turn left on **Hood Street** (unmarked).

22.5 At a T-intersection with **Bluff Road**, turn right. Excellent views of Mount Hood and the Sandy River Gorge are available at mile 23.4. Watch for rafters and kayakers in the river below.

25.7 Turn right on **Hudson Road**, which makes a steep descent starting a half mile later. Be careful on this narrow, relatively rough road. (For those of you tiring of all the hills, a flat shortcut is available here. Continue west on Bluff Road, then turn right on Cottrell Road at mile 27.5, rejoining the main route at its mile 30.0. The shortcut reduces the length of the ride by 1.2 miles.)

26.9 Turn left at a T-intersection with **Lusted Road**. (Dodge Park is located about a mile to the right, down a steep hill.) Lusted Road is level for 2.5 miles, then climbs out of the gorge.

30.2 Turn right on **Hosner Road**.

30.7 Turn left on **Oxbow Parkway**. (To make a side trip into Oxbow Park, go straight, down another long hill.) Follow Oxbow Parkway as it eventually becomes **Division Street**.

33.2 Turn right on **302nd Avenue**, which turns left at mile 34.2 and becomes **Kerslake Road**.

35.0 Turn left on **Sweetbriar Road** one block before an intersection with Stark Street. Follow Sweetbriar through an intersection with Strebin Road at mile 35.4.

36.1 Turn right on **Troutdale Road**. Follow it into Troutdale as it becomes **Sandy Street**, then turns into **Third Street**.

38.3 Turn right on **Harlow Street**.

38.4 Turn right on **East Columbia Street**, and follow it to the Troutdale bridge at 39.1 miles.

39.2 Cross the bridge and turn left.

39.4 Lewis and Clark State Park. Turn right into the parking lot. End of ride.

Multnomah County

4 SAUVIE ISLAND

Starting Point: A gravel parking lot at the east end of the Sauvie Island Bridge, 12 miles north of Portland, just east of U.S. Highway 30.
Distance: 12.4 miles.
Terrain: Flat.
Total Cumulative Elevation Gain: Negligible.
Recommended Time of Year: Any season.

Recommended Starting Time: Anytime.
Allow: 1 to 2 hours.
Points of Interest
Sauvie Island Wildlife
  Management Area
Walton Beach
Bybee-Howell House

The loop road around the southern end of Sauvie Island is probably the single most popular backroads bike trip in the state. It is also very popular with long-distance runners. The reasons are obvious. The island is only a dozen miles from downtown Portland, yet it is scenic, historic, teeming with wildlife, and (above all else) perfectly level.

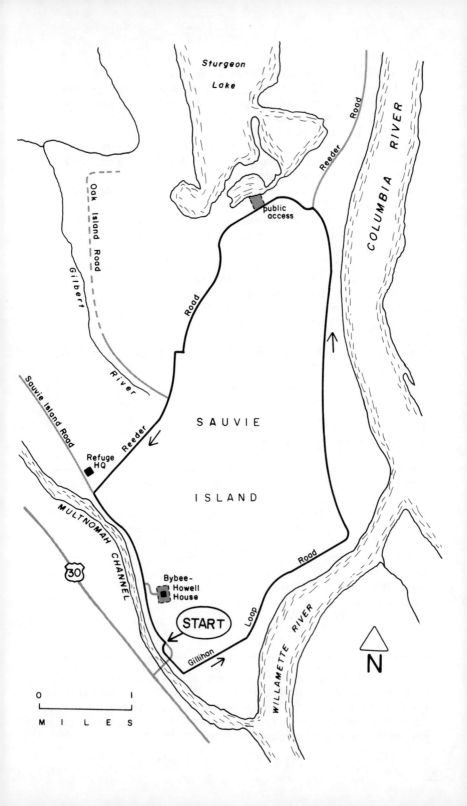

One of the largest freshwater islands in the country, Sauvie Island sits in the mouth of the Willamette. The Columbia forms its eastern boundary, while the Multnomah Channel winds past its twenty-mile-long western shore. Sailboats populate the Columbia, houseboats line Multnomah Channel, and huge cargo ships steam up and down the Willamette.

The island is only a few feet above sea level, and if the southern end were not diked, the entire island would be under water several times a year. As a result of the diking, the southern end is now rich farmland. The northern end remains covered to a large extent with the waters of Sturgeon Lake and the Gilbert River (yes, Sauvie Island is large enough to have its own rivers and lakes, and those lakes in turn have their own islands).

Much of the northern end is a state wildlife management area. A major stopping point on the Pacific flyway, Sauvie Island is prime bird-watching country. In spring and fall, flocks of sandhill cranes stop by on their way north or south, and great blue herons can be seen year around. Stop by the management area headquarters on Sauvie Island Road for brochures on the wildlife of the island and an excellent map.

Sauvie Island has a rich history. Lewis and Clark camped on the island but failed to notice that a major river, the Willamette, joined the Columbia at the southern end of the island. Later the island was used as a dairy farm by the Hudson's Bay Company and came to be named after a French-Canadian employee of the dairy. In 1856, a stately home was built on the west side of the island by James Bybee. The house still stands and is held open to the public every summer by the Oregon Historical Society. Each fall, usually on the last Saturday in September, the Society holds a "wintering-in" festival at the house to celebrate the island's harvest and the changing of the seasons.

The main 12.4-mile loop around the southern end of the island is described below, but three side trips can be followed toward the north end of the island. At mile 6.1, Reeder Road leads north eight miles to Walton Beach on the Columbia. At mile 9.2, Oak Island Road follows the Gilbert River toward Sturgeon Lake, while at mile 10.5, Sauvie Island Road can be followed north along Multnomah Channel.

One caution: the island's roads are narrow, and the residents are understandably impatient with inconsiderate bikers and joggers. When traffic is present, ride single file. It's just common courtesy.

MILEAGE LOG

0.0 East end of the Sauvie Island Bridge (store). Ride south, under the bridge, on **Gillihan Loop Road**.

6.1 Turn left at an intersection with Reeder Road. (For a side trip to Walton Beach, turn right.) At mile 7.3, a set of stairs leads over a dike for watching birds on Sturgeon Lake.

9.2 Keep left at an intersection with Oak Island Road.

10.5 At a T-intersection, turn left on **Gillihan Loop Road**. (For a side trip north along Multnomah Channel, turn right on Sauvie Island Road.)

11.5 The Bybee-Howell House is on the left, down a short driveway.

12.4 East end of the Sauvie Island Bridge. End of ride.

Multnomah County

5 SKYLINE BOULEVARD

Starting Point: Willamette Stone State Park, at 6500 N.W. Skyline Boulevard in Portland. From downtown Portland, drive west on West Burnside Street then bear right on Skyline Boulevard.
Distance: 33.2 miles.
Terrain: Very hilly.
Total Cumulative Elevation Gain: 2900 feet.
Recommended Time of Year: Any season.
Recommended Starting Time: Before 11:00 A.M.
Allow: 4 hours.

Points of Interest
Willamette Stone State Park
Forest Park

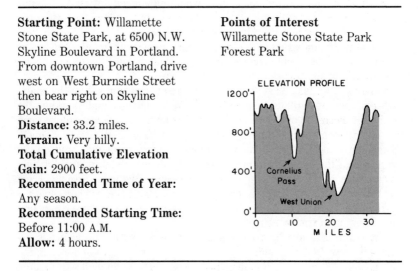

The Tualatin Mountains form a thin ridge that stretches along the Willamette River from Portland northwest toward Sauvie Island, separating the lower Willamette from the Tualatin Valley to the west. For years the ridge served as an obstacle to Tualatin Valley farmers who needed to bring their crops to market at shipping ports such as Linnton and Portland. Eventually the ridge was crossed by several roads, with colorful names such as Canyon, Logie Trail, and Rocky Point.

Many of the road names on the ridge are Teutonic in origin, since the Tualatin Valley was a popular settling place for German immigrants. While other Teutonic street names in the Portland area were changed during World War I, the ridge still boasts Germantown Road, Kaiser Road, and Saltzman Road.

One road, appropriately named Skyline Boulevard, was built on the long crest of the ridge, running 20 miles from Burnside Street to 1609-foot Dixie Mountain. This ride follows that road for most of its length, then drops into the Tualatin Valley for the return trip. It is a hilly ride, since the

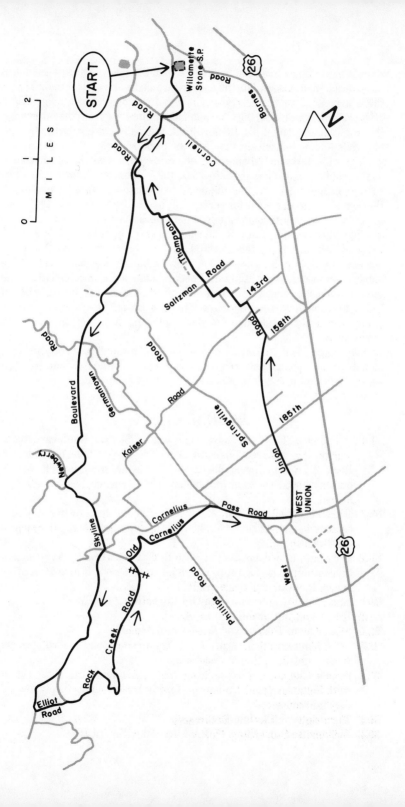

ridge is more than a thousand feet higher than the valley floor and is notched by several small passes, but the scenery is unsurpassed. The road follows the true crest of the ridge, so views in both directions reward the pedaler's effort. To the southwest, the Chehalem Mountains rise from the far edge of the flat Tualatin Valley. To the northeast, the Willamette joins the Columbia while Mount St. Helens stands in the background.

The ride starts at Willamette Stone State Park near the southern end of the ridge. Originally marked in 1851, the Willamette Stone is the intersection of the Willamette Meridian and the Willamette Baseline and is still the central reference point for surveys of the Pacific Northwest. The stone is just a short walk through the woods from Skyline Boulevard.

For the first nine miles of the ride, much of the northeast side of the ridge is part of Forest Park, a 4700-acre preserve that is said to be the largest city park in the country. The wooded hillside was once platted as a subdivision in the city of Linnton. Portland annexed Linnton in 1915, and later the hillside land was turned over to the city due to nonpayment of taxes and was officially designated a park in 1947. The city has refrained from intensively developing the park, allowing it to remain an urban wilderness.

The ridge itself is a mixture of wooded hills, small pastures, an occasional store or grange hall, and a growing number of houses, but mainly it seems lofty and isolated, protected by its steep ramparts.

MILEAGE LOG

0.0 Willamette Stone State Park. Ride west on **Skyline Boulevard**, passing through intersections with Cornell Road (1.4 miles), Thompson Road (2.3 miles), Springville Road (5.1 miles), Germantown Road (6.2 miles), Newberry Road (8.9 miles), and Cornelius Pass Road (10.6 miles).

14.1 Turn left on **Elliot Road**. A few feet after this intersection, the ride crosses its highest point (1190 feet) and then starts its rapid drop into the Tualatin Valley.

14.8 Turn right at a T-intersection with **Rock Creek Road**. The road continues to drop rapidly until it crosses Rock Creek at mile 16.4, after which the decline is more gradual.

19.1 Make a hard right turn onto **Old Cornelius Pass Road**.

21.2 Turn right on **Cornelius Pass Road**.

22.7 West Union. Turn left on **West Union Road**.

26.7 At a T-intersection, turn left on **Thompson Road** (143rd Avenue heads right from the intersection).

27.7 Follow Thompson Road as it jogs right, then left, at an intersection with Saltzman Road. Thompson Road begins to climb steeply toward Skyline Boulevard.

30.9 Turn right on **Skyline Boulevard**.

33.2 Willamette Stone State Park on the right. End of ride.

6 FARMINGTON-SCHOLLS LOOP

Starting Point: Hazeldale
School, 20080 Farmington Road,
four miles west of Beaverton on
Farmington Road (State
Highway 10).
Distance: 19.7 miles.
Terrain: Flat with some
moderate hills.
**Total Cumulative Elevation
Gain:** 450 feet.
Recommended Time of Year:
Any season.
Recommended Starting Time:
Before 1:00 P.M.
Allow: 2 hours.

Points of Interest
Tualatin Valley
Vineyards and wineries

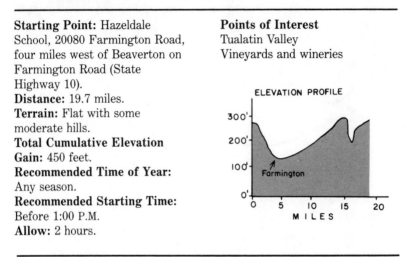

This short route circles an historic area of the Tualatin Valley and crosses
the Tualatin River at the former sites of two ferries of pioneer days. The
short length of the ride and its proximity to Portland make it an ideal afternoon outing.

The ride starts in Hazeldale, less than four miles west of Beaverton, on
Farmington Road. Because a bike lane extends along Farmington Road
from Beaverton to beyond Hazeldale, the starting point is easily accessible
by bike from the metropolitan area.

From Hazeldale, the route follows Farmington Road west along the
northern edge of Cooper Mountain. At Farmington, the road crosses the
river via Harris Bridge. Just a few feet south of the bridge, evidence of an
old ferry landing can still be seen.

Farmington, like most of the towns along this route, is nearly nonexistent. A church and store once stood west of the bridge, but today both
are gone and a tavern on the river's east bank seems to have replaced them
as the center of the community. Other "towns" along the route include
Midway, Scholls, North Scholls, and Kinton.

North of Scholls, another historic ferry crossing has been replaced by a
bridge. For many years Scholls Ferry was operated by Peter Scholl, a pioneer of 1847. His ferry was a few feet downstream from the present bridge;
the remains of a previous bridge can often be seen during low water.

This route is relatively flat due to the level floor of the Tualatin Valley. In
the 20 rivermiles between Scholls and the Lake Oswego area, the bed of the
Tualatin River drops only 18 inches as it follows its meandering course
downstream.

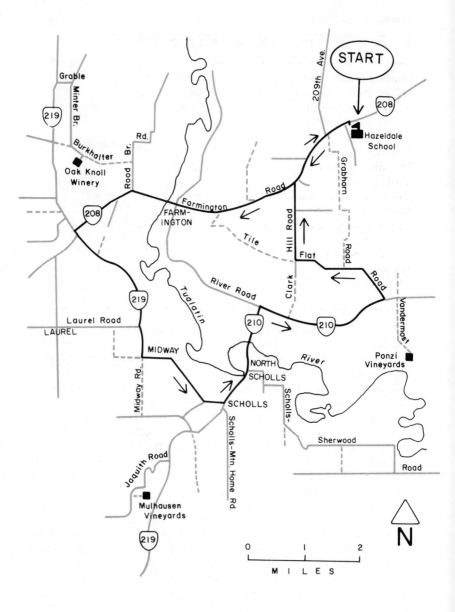

START

Grable

219

Minter Br.

Burkhalter

Rood Br. Rd.

Oak Knoll
Winery

208

Farmington

FARM-
INGTON

Tile

Road

Clark Hill Road

Flat

209th Ave.

Grabhorn

Road

208

Hazeldale
School

River Road

219

Laurel Road

LAUREL

Tualatin

MIDWAY

Midway Rd.

210

NORTH
SCHOLLS

SCHOLLS

210

River

Scholls-

Vandermost

Road

Ponzi
Vineyards

Jaquith Road

Mulhausen
Vineyards

219

Scholls-Mtn. Home Rd.

Sherwood

Road

0   1   2

M I L E S

N

Due to its fine farmland, the Tualatin Valley attracted some of Oregon's first settlers. For the same reason, in recent years it has attracted some of Oregon's first vineyards and wineries. Many acres of wine grapes have been planted in the valley in the last few years, particularly on the slopes of the Chehalem Mountains immediately southwest of this route.

At least three wineries have been developed near the route and are marked on the route map. The wineries are generally open to the public on weekend afternoons, and they maintain small tasting rooms and picnic areas. Visiting any of the three shown on the map involves travelling short sections of gravel roads, and one (Mulhausen Vineyards) is located near the summit of the steep Chehalem Mountains. If all three are visited, the length of the ride increases to about 30 miles, and four or five hours will be needed to complete the tour. If you have the time and the energy, visits to the wineries are very worthwhile, but don't overindulge—you and your bike must get home safely.

MILEAGE LOG

0.0 Hazeldale School. Ride west on **Farmington Road** (Highway 208).

5.7 Turn left at a T-intersection with **Highway 219** and follow it south.

10.4 Scholls (store). Turn left on **Highway 210** (Scholls Ferry Road).

11.2 North Scholls (store). Continue northbound.

12.2 Follow Highway 210 (Scholls Ferry Road) when it turns right at an intersection with River Road.

14.7 Turn left on **Tile Flat Road**.

16.7 Turn right at an unmarked intersection (**Clark Hill Road**).

18.1 Turn right at a T-intersection with **Highway 208** (Farmington Road).

19.7 Hazeldale School. End of ride.

7 LOWER TUALATIN VALLEY

Starting Point: Tualatin City Park, on State Highway 212 just north of Boones Ferry Road in Tualatin. From I-5, drive west from exit 289 on Nyberg Road, then turn north on Tualatin Avenue. Use the northernmost of the park entrances and park in the lot north of the railroad trestle.
Distance: 34.4 miles.
Terrain: Generally flat with some moderate hills.
Total Cumulative Elevation Gain: 1100 feet.
Recommended Time of Year: Any season.
Recommended Starting Time: 10:00 A.M.
Allow: 4 hours.

Points of Interest
Tualatin River

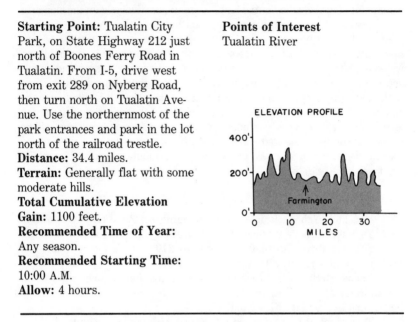

The rich, flat farmland of the Tualatin Valley attracted some of Oregon's earliest settlers. Primitive roads soon crisscrossed the broad valley, allowing the grain to be hauled to market. Farmers with property along the river soon realized that a steady income could be generated by operating ferries, since bridges were nonexistent.

Many of the roads on this ride still carry names reflecting the routes to those ferries. Boones Ferry Road leads south to the site of the ferry that operated on the Willamette at Wilsonville for more than 110 years. Scholls Ferry Road still crosses the Tualatin near the donation land claim Peter Scholl first settled in 1847, although a modern bridge now stands where the ferry ran.

The Tualatin River is extremely flat. This ride crosses the river at rivermile 9 (measured from the river's mouth) and again at rivermile 33, yet in the interval the riverbed gains only 10 feet of elevation. The Tualatin is also a very twisted river; those 24 miles of river require only about 17 miles of pedaling on relatively straight roads, and that same distance is only 10 miles as the crow flies.

The roads along the Tualatin, however, are not nearly as flat as the river itself. Although the southern half of the ride (the return leg) is fairly flat, the northern half is relatively hilly, particularly on Beef Bend Road, which traverses the south side of Bull Mountain. The hills are hardly long or steep, however, and the views of the valley make the effort worthwhile.

The lower Tualatin Valley is popular bike country, since it is scenic, free of most traffic, and readily accessible to Portland riders. Although the route described here starts in Tualatin, many of the riders encountered will be making round trips from Portland or Beaverton.

The ride starts at Tualatin City Park, one of two parks the city of Tualatin maintains on the river. This park is noted as the site of a crawfish festival, held each year in August, at which the guest of honor is also the main dish. When the festival originated several years ago, the crawfish were caught in the Tualatin, but the festival has since increased in size, and the crawfish population of the river has dropped, so the tiny freshwater lobsters are now trucked in from central Oregon.

MILEAGE LOG

0.0 Tualatin City Park. Leave the park and proceed south on **Tualatin Avenue** (Highway 212). A narrow bike path lies along the east side of the road.

0.2 Turn left on **Boones Ferry Road**. In a few blocks, the road curves left (north) and crosses the Tualatin River. At mile 0.8, continue straight through an intersection with Lower Boones Ferry Road.

1.8 Turn left on **Durham Road**. Parts of Durham Road have no

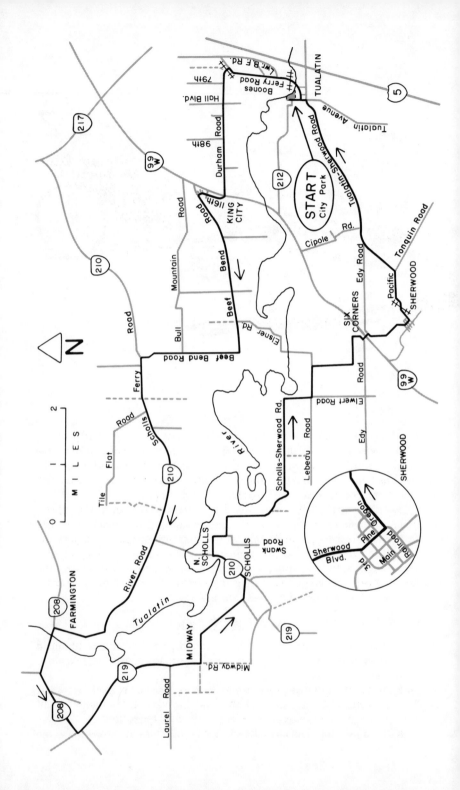

shoulders, so ride carefully. A bike path begins at mile 2.5, but it is narrow and poorly maintained.

4.0 King City (store). Durham Road crosses Highway 99W and becomes **116th Avenue**. Cross Highway 99W, then follow 116th as it turns north and passes through the middle of a shopping center. At mile 4.3, 116th curves northwest through a residential area.

4.4 Turn left (west) at a T-intersection with **Beef Bend Road**. At mile 7.3 the road turns north.

9.1 T-intersection with **Scholls Ferry Road** (Highway 210). Turn left.

12.4 Go straight on **River Road**, leaving Highway 210 when it turns left at an intersection near two interesting old houses. (For those who prefer a shorter ride, turn left at this intersection and follow Highway 219 south 1.1 miles to North Scholls, which is listed below at mile 22.7. By taking this shortcut, the total length of the ride is shortened by 9.2 miles, from 34.4 miles to 25.2 miles.)

15.2 Farmington. Turn left on **Highway 208**. At mile 15.3, the road crosses the Tualatin River.

17.3 Turn left at a T-intersection with **Highway 219**.

20.1 Midway. Follow Highway 219 as it turns left.

22.0 Scholls (store). Turn left on **Scholls Ferry Road** (Highway 210).

22.7 North Scholls (store). Turn right (east) on **Scholls-Sherwood Road** and follow it as it works its way south and east toward Sherwood. At mile 23.2, do not go straight on Swank Road, but follow Scholls-Sherwood Road as it turns. Similar intersections occur at miles 26.9 and 27.4.

28.6 Six Corners. Cross Highway 99W, then bear right on **Sherwood Boulevard**.

29.4 Sherwood. Sherwood Boulevard ends at an intersection with Pine Street and Third Avenue. Bear left on **Pine Street**.

29.5 Turn left on **Oregon Street**. At mile 29.9, Oregon Street turns right, becomes **Pacific Street**, and eventually becomes **Tualatin-Sherwood Road**.

33.8 Intersection with **Tualatin Avenue**. Turn left, being particularly careful on this busy street.

34.3 When Tualatin Avenue (Highway 212) turns left, go straight, into Tualatin City Park.

34.4 Tualatin City Park. End of ride.

8   NORTH TUALATIN VALLEY

Starting Point: Corner of Ninth Avenue and Maple Street in Hillsboro, on the north side of Shute Park.
Distance: 35.3 miles.
Terrain: Flat with one steep hill.
Total Cumulative Elevation Gain: 750 feet.
Recommended Time of Year: Any season.
Recommended Starting Time: Before 11:00 A.M.
Allow: 4 hours.

Points of Interest
Shute Park
Pacific University
Verboort

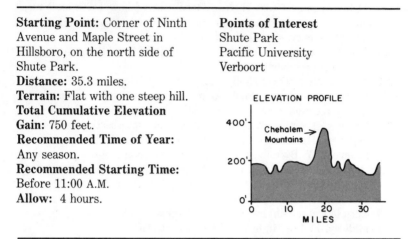

ELEVATION PROFILE

Although the Tualatin River has a very crooked and meandering course, it has shaped a graceful crescent valley as it flows north from Yamhill County, curves around the north end of the Chehalem Mountains, then flows south to meet the Willamette near West Linn. The ride described here circles the northernmost section of that crescent, visiting the towns of Hillsboro, Cornelius, and Forest Grove, as well as several smaller communities.

Like the river itself, the ride is flat, with the exception of one short (but steep) detour over the northern toe of the Chehalem Mountains. Since it passes through several towns, the ride has some moderate traffic spots, but not enough to detract from the pleasure of pedaling the lonely farm roads that make up the rest of the ride.

The tour starts in Hillsboro, the county seat, then proceeds out among the farms northwest of town. After passing through a residential section of Cornelius, the route eventually reaches the tiny community of Verboort. Because it is so far from any main roads, one cannot imagine travellers passing through Verboort on their way to anywhere else. It is the home of a sausage festival held in early November each year and is a predominantly Catholic community made up of Dutch immigrants who first settled in Wisconsin before moving on to Oregon. Don't expect the town store to be open on Sunday.

West of Verboort, the route follows State Highway 47 south through Forest Grove, a pretty town which grew up around the shady campus of Pacific University. When the school was founded in the 1840s, the area was known as West Tualatin Plains, while Hillsboro was referred to as East Tualatin Plains.

The route continues on Highway 47 for three miles south of Forest Grove, then turns southeast and crosses the Tualatin River. The northern toe of the Chehalem Mountains is surmounted by climbing a very steep hill and is left by way of a rapid descent to the valley floor.

The remainder of the ride follows the river south to the Farmington area, then follows River Road north into Hillsboro. The last few miles have some moderate traffic, so ride carefully.

Local roads offer several opportunities for shortening the 35.3-mile ride described here. The best such opportunity occurs at mile 24.3, where rather than turning south on State Highway 219 toward Farmington, turning left will return the rider to Hillsboro in about three miles, shortening the ride by about six miles. In addition, a left turn on Long Road at mile 5.3 will shorten the route by about 2.2 miles, although Long Road has some gravel sections.

MILEAGE LOG

0.0 Corner of Ninth Avenue and Maple Street in Hillsboro. Proceed north on **Ninth Avenue**.

0.1 Turn left on **Walnut Street**.

0.7 Turn right on **2nd Avenue**.

1.1 Turn left (west) on **Main Street**. Main Street is one-way west at this point but becomes two-way one block later.

1.4 Turn right on **Connell Avenue**. At mile 2.1, Connell Avenue curves to the west, then becomes **Hornecker Road**.

4.8 Turn left at a T-intersection with **Susbauer Road**.

6.5 Turn right on **Davis Street**.

7.0 At a T-intersection with **10th Avenue**, turn right (north). In a few blocks, 10th Avenue becomes **Cornelius-Schefflin Road**. At mile 9.0, the road turns to the west.

9.1 Cornelius-Schefflin Road turns north. Go straight (west) on **Verboort Road**.

10.0 Verboort. Continue west on Verboort Road.

11.1 Turn left (south) on **Highway 47**. Watch carefully for traffic. At mile 12.3, the highway enters Forest Grove. Lincoln Park is on the right side of the road at mile 12.6.

12.8 Follow Highway 47 as it turns right on **University Avenue**, then left on **College Way**. Pacific University is on the left.

13.2 Turn right on **Pacific Avenue**, then left on **B Street**, following Highway 47.

14.6 Highway 47 joins the **Tualatin Valley Highway**. Bear right (south). A bike path starts on the right side of the highway at this intersection, then ends at mile 15.0. At mile 15.4, the highway passes through the outskirts of the small town of Dilley.

16.3 Carefully cross Highway 47 and turn left on **Springhill Road**. At

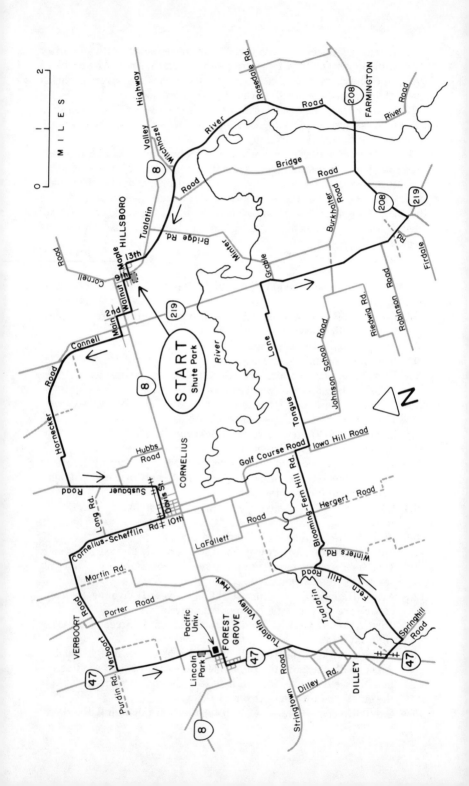

mile 16.7, the road crosses the Tualatin River.

16.8 Turn left on **Fern Hill Road**. This level road travels northeast along the north end of the Chehalem Mountains.

18.9 Turn right on **Blooming-Fern Hill Road**, which climbs 200 feet in the next 0.4 mile. About a mile later, the road drops back down into the valley.

21.1 Turn right (south) at a T-intersection with **Golf Course Road**.

21.4 T-intersection with **Tongue Lane**. Turn left.

24.3 Turn right at a T-intersection with **Highway 219**. (For those preferring a shorter ride, a left turn at this intersection will return the rider to Hillsboro in about three miles.)

27.3 Turn left on **Highway 208** (Farmington Road). At mile 29.2, the road crosses the Tualatin River.

29.3 Farmington. Turn left on **River Road**. At mile 33.2, Witch Hazel Road joins from the right (east). At mile 33.5, at an intersection with Rood Bridge Road, sidewalks begin on both sides of the road, with the sidewalk on the left (southwest) side of the road designated as a bike route. Due to the volume of traffic on this part of River Road, the bike route is the safest approach.

34.7 Intersection with Tualatin Valley Highway (Highway 8). Cross the highway and proceed north on **13th Avenue**.

35.0 Turn left on **Maple Street**. At mile 35.2, follow Maple Street west across Tualatin Valley Highway.

35.3 Corner of Maple Street and Ninth Avenue. End of ride.

9 MOUNTAINDALE

Starting Point: West Union School, 12 miles west of Portland. From U.S. Highway 26, turn north on Helvetia Road and drive north one mile, then turn left on West Union Road to the school.
Distance: 22.3 miles.
Terrain: Flat.
Total Cumulative Elevation Gain: 250 feet.
Recommended Time of Year: Any season.
Recommended Starting Time: Before noon.
Allow: 2 or 3 hours.

Points of Interest
Mountaindale
Glider flights

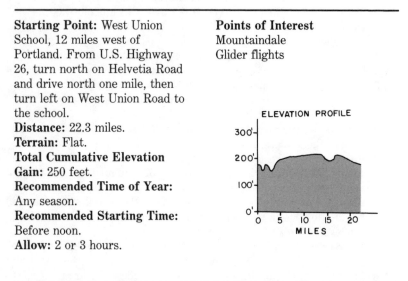

ELEVATION PROFILE

When the Oregon Country's first government was formed in 1843, one of its initial tasks was to divide the region into counties. Of the four counties created that year, the one named Twality stretched from the Willamette River west to the Pacific and from the Yamhill River north into what is now Washington State.

The name Twality was short-lived, as was the sweeping size of the county. Within one year the county began to be divided into smaller counties, and within six years the name was changed to Washington County. A derivative of the name, however, is still applied to the river that drains nearly all of Washington County.

A bicycle ride through present-day Washington County is normally a leisurely affair, particularly when the route is restricted to the level Tualatin Valley farmland in the central part of the county and avoids the hills that make up the outlying areas. This route is such a ride. It starts north of Hillsboro, then travels west and north to the base of the Tualatin Mountains, then proceeds southeast, skirting the base of the mountains, being particularly careful not to enter the hills.

Flat doesn't equal dull, however, for the scenery is superb. The southern half of the ride traverses pastoral farmland, and the northern half passes through a variety of woods and pastures. Midway through the ride, a lunch stop at the Mountaindale store is most appropriate. The store celebrated its hundredth birthday in 1982, although the present building is a mere 97 years old. Like many small-town stores (in this case the store *is* the town), the

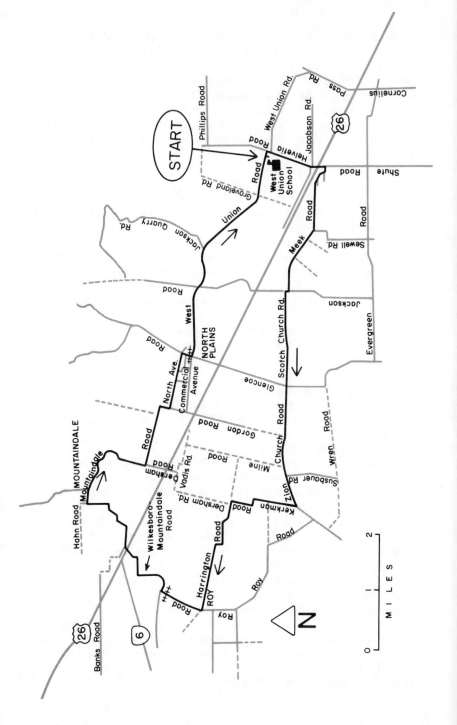

55

Mountaindale store sells everything from soup to nuts and from food to feed.

As long as you are watching the scenery, don't forget to watch the skies. With at least four airfields located along the route, the skies are crowded, particularly on sunny days. The busiest of the airfields is Hillsboro Airport, about two miles northeast of Hillsboro. The most interesting of the airfields, located south of the route near mile 16, specializes in glider flights. Take a few minutes to watch the tow plane spiral up into the sky with a glider on the end of its cable, and try to spot the glider as it swoops in silently to land.

MILEAGE LOG

0.0 West Union School. Leave the parking lot and turn right (east) on **West Union Road**.

0.1 Bear right at an intersection with **Helvetia Road** and follow it south.

1.0 Carefully cross U.S. 26, after which Helvetia Road becomes **Shute Road**. (In 1984, this intersection was scheduled to be reconstructed into a two-level interchange.)

1.1 Turn right on **Meek Road** and follow it as it bears right, then parallels U.S. 26.

3.6 Turn right at a T-intersection with **Jackson Road**.

3.7 Turn left (west) on **Scotch Church Road**. After passing through an intersection with Glencoe Road at mile 5.4, Scotch Church Road becomes **Zion Church Road**.

7.5 Turn right on **Kerkman Road**.

8.7 At a T-intersection, turn left onto **Harrington Road** (unmarked).

10.7 Roy. You can't miss St. Francis Church, but also note its matching mailbox.

10.8 Turn right on **Roy Road**.

11.6 Turn right at a T-intersection with **Wilkesboro-Mountaindale Road**.

12.8 Carefully cross Sunset Highway (U.S. 26), then turn right on **Mountaindale Road**. At mile 13.9, follow Mountaindale Road as it turns right at an intersection with Hahn Road.

14.4 Mountaindale (store). Continue straight (east) on Mountaindale Road. About a mile later, Mountaindale Road turns south.

16.0 Follow Mountaindale Road by turning left (east). Dersham Road continues straight (south).

17.0 Mountaindale Road turns south and becomes **Gordon Road**.

17.2 Turn left on **North Avenue**.

18.2 Turn right on **Glencoe Road**.

18.4 After crossing some railroad tracks, turn left on **Commercial Avenue**, which soon becomes **West Union Road**. Follow this road east, through intersections with Jackson Road and Jackson Quarry Road.

22.3 West Union School. End of Ride.

10 GALES CREEK

Starting Point: Rogers Park at the corner of Douglas Street and 17th Avenue in Forest Grove (two blocks south of Highway 8 on Douglas Street). Park on the south side of the park (17th Avenue).
Distance: 25.6 miles.
Terrain: Moderately flat; some hills.
Total Cumulative Elevation Gain: 550 feet.
Recommended Time of Year: Any season.
Recommended Starting Time: Noon.
Allow: 3 hours.

Points of Interest
Forest Grove
Gales Creek Valley
Vineyards and wineries

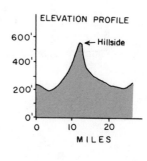

Dairy Creek and Gales Creek are two of the largest tributaries of the Tualatin River. Dairy Creek, named for a Hudson's Bay Company dairy that once operated on its banks, is the only Tualatin tributary that has been navigated: in the 1800s steamboats frequently used Dairy Creek to call on a flour mill at the now nonexistent town of Centerville.

Gales Creek, on the other hand, was named for an Oregon pioneer who was no friend of the Hudson's Bay Company. In 1842 Joseph Gale drove nearly five thousand head of livestock from California to the Willamette Valley, effectively destroying the livestock monopoly held by the H.B.C. He later served as one of three commissioners named to head the first Oregon Provisional Government.

This ride visits the valleys of both Dairy Creek and Gales Creek and crosses the ridge that separates them. It starts at Rogers Park, which occupies a full city block in the center of Forest Grove, a shady little college town. From Forest Grove, the route heads north on State Highway 47 (watch for moderate traffic) into the flat farmland of the Dairy Creek Valley. The route eventually turns west and begins a gentle climb into the rolling foothills. In the transition, the surroundings change from broad fields to nurseries and small woodlots.

The route crosses the ridge near the community of Hillside, then follows a series of steep curves into the Gales Creek Valley. In contrast to the broad valley of Dairy Creek, Gales Creek Valley is narrow with sloping

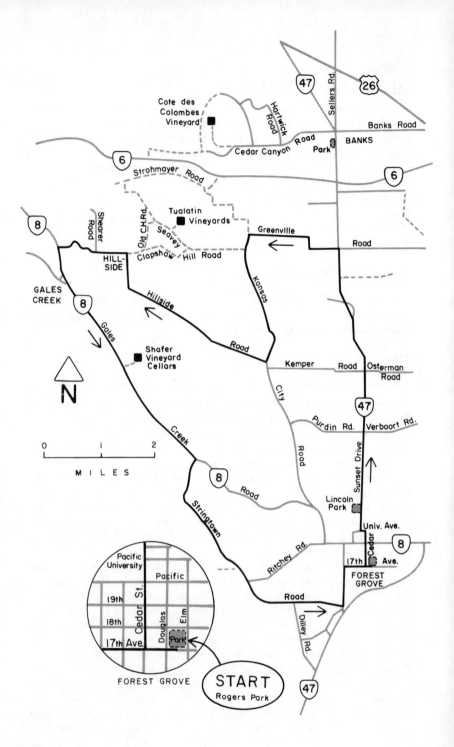

wooded sides. The floor of the valley is relatively flat, and the last few miles of the ride seem to glide by with little effort. The route follows State Highway 8 (Gales Creek Road) but makes a slight detour near Forest Grove to take advantage of quiet Stringtown Road.

The hills surrounding Dairy and Gales creeks contain a number of vineyards, which produce wine grapes for the Willamette Valley's burgeoning wine industry. The hills also contain three wineries, which are shown on the tour map. All three invite the public to sample their wares in their tasting rooms and to picnic on their grounds. Although one of the wineries (Shafer Vineyard Cellars) is located only a few hundred yards from the route, the other two are several miles off it, at the end of gravel roads. A route visiting all three would require perhaps five hours to cover the 30 or 40 miles involved. While the wineries offer a fascinating look at small-scale production of fine wines, bicyclists must remember that the combination of wine tasting and bike touring must be approached with caution.

MILEAGE LOG

0.0 Rogers Park in Forest Grove. From the parking lot on the south side of the park, turn right (west) on **17th Avenue**.

0.1 Turn right (north) on **Cedar Street**.

0.6 Pacific University is on the left. Turn left on **University Avenue**.

0.7 Turn right on **Sunset Drive** (Highway 47), and follow it north for several miles.

5.8 Turn left on **Greenville Road** (unmarked; a sign points to Kansas City).

7.6 At a T-intersection, turn left on **Kansas City Road**.

10.1 Turn right on **Hillside Road**.

13.6 Hillside. An 1884 church stands just east of this intersection. Turn left on **Clapshaw Hill Road**. Follow it through an intersection with Shearer Road at mile 14.1, after which the road drops steeply into the Gales Creek Valley.

15.0 Turn left at a T-intersection with **Highway 8** (Gales Creek Road). The road passes through the small town of Gales Creek (store) at mile 16.6.

19.7 Turn right on **Stringtown Road**.

24.2 Intersection with **Highway 47**. Turn left.

25.0 Turn right on **17th Avenue**.

25.6 Rogers Park. End of ride.

11 HAGG LAKE

Starting Point: Scoggins Valley Park. From Forest Grove, drive south on State Highway 47 for 4.5 miles, then turn right on Scoggins Valley Road. After entering the park, leave your car at the overlook area at Recreation Area A East.
Distance: 11.0 miles.
Terrain: Moderately hilly.
Total Cumulative Elevation Gain: 750 feet.
Recommended Time of Year: Any season.
Recommended Starting Time: Anytime.
Allow: 1 or 2 hours.

Points of Interest
Henry Hagg Lake
Scoggins Dam
Scoggins Valley Park

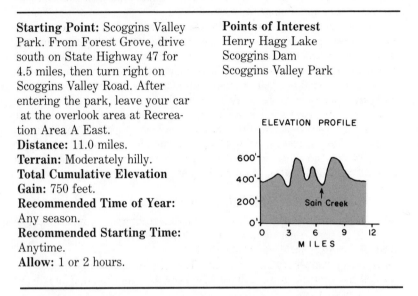

ELEVATION PROFILE

Washington County maps printed as recently as the early 1970s show a secluded valley a few miles northwest of Gaston. Scoggins Valley Road is shown leading west along Scoggins Creek, through a gap in the foothills, into a small valley of level farmland. In the middle of the valley, where four streams came together, Forest Dale School is shown sitting next to a small church.

Today, Forest Dale School, if it is still there, stands under 50 feet of water, as does most of Scoggins Valley, because of the construction of an earthen dam in 1974 by the Bureau of Reclamation. The large reservoir formed by the dam, Henry Hagg Lake, holds nearly sixty thousand acre-feet of water for flood control, irrigation, and recreation.

The shores of the lake are now a large park and are circled by a road that makes a fine bike route. The road follows the perimeter of the lake and also crosses the half-mile long dam. Along the way, it passes several viewpoints, picnic areas, and short trails. Pack a lunch and let your hunger pangs determine your stopping point.

Although the Hagg Lake route is hilly, its length is ideal for families or others who prefer shorter rides. During good spring and summer weather, however, the road is heavily travelled by motorists, particularly those with boat trailers. The shoulder is wide, but watch for traffic, especially when riding with children.

Washington County has few large parks, and even fewer lakes, so Scoggins Valley Park and Hagg Lake see heavy and diverse use. Water skiers dominate the southeastern end of the lake in such numbers that park rules

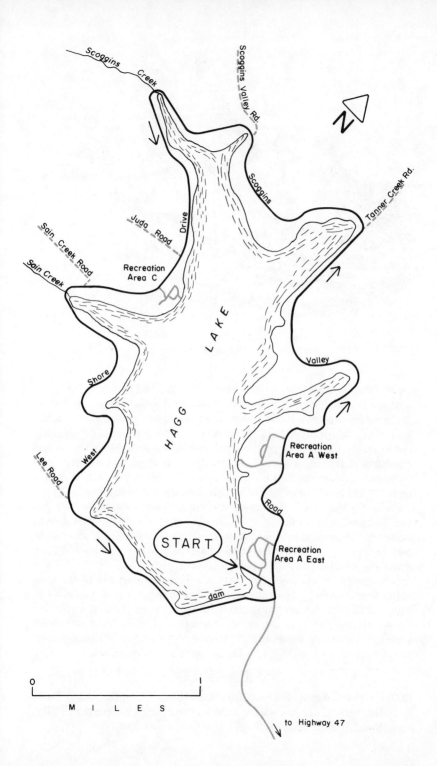

Scoggins Creek

Scoggins Valley Rd.

Scoggins

Tanner Creek Rd.

Juda Road

Drive

Sain Creek Road

Sain Creek

Recreation Area C

Valley

Shore

HAGG LAKE

West

Lee Road

Recreation Area A West

Road

START

Recreation Area A East

dam

to Highway 47

0   1

M I L E S

*Call the county road department
to see if the road is still there...*

require counter-clockwise travel on the water to avoid collisions, while the upper end of the lake is reserved for "low wake" activities such as fishing and canoeing. The entire lake is sometimes reserved for boat races, water-rescue training, or other uses. In addition to motorists and bicyclists, joggers often use the road for training, and triathalon participants have taken advantage of the lake and road for swimming, cycling, and running.

The only problem with the road is caused by Mother Nature. Perhaps upset at the loss of her pretty valley, she keeps pushing large pieces of the road into the lake. The latest series of seven cave-ins was repaired, and the road reopened, in the fall of 1983. The county hopes these most recent repairs will be permanent, but prospective bicyclists might call the county road department at 648-8784 or the park headquarters at 359-5732 to determine whether or not the road is still there.

Although the road is open all year, the park facilities are closed each winter from October 31 to the opening day of fishing season in late April. The water level also drops late in the fall to make room for winter rains, so the best seasons to visit are spring through early fall. Naturally, those same seasons are popular with boaters and motorists. When the park facilities are open, a small fee is charged at the park entrance.

MILEAGE LOG

0.0 Overlook area at Recreation Area A East of Scoggins Valley Park. Ride out of the recreation area and turn left on **Scoggins Valley Road**. The right shoulder of the road is a bike lane.

0.9 On the left is the entrance to Recreation Area A West.

4.4 When Scoggins Valley Road turns right and becomes gravel, continue straight on **West Shore Drive**.

4.8 The bike lane crosses from the right side of the road to the left.

5.2 The road crosses Scoggins Creek on a narrow bridge. Watch carefully for traffic.

6.4 On the left is the entrance to Recreation Area C.

7.1 Bridge over Sain Creek.

9.8 The road starts to cross Scoggins Dam.

10.6 Turn left at a T-intersection with **Scoggins Valley Road**.

10.8 Turn left into Recreation Area A East.

11.0 Overlook area. End of ride.

Clackamas County
12 LOLO PASS

Starting Point: Zigzag Ranger Station (Mount Hood National Forest) in Zigzag, 40 miles east of Portland on U.S. Highway 26.
Distance: 24.2 miles.
Terrain: Very hilly.
Total Cumulative Elevation Gain: 2500 feet.
Recommended Time of Year: Spring through fall.
Recommended Starting Time: Before noon.
Allow: 3 hours.

Points of Interest
Views of Mount Hood
French's Dome

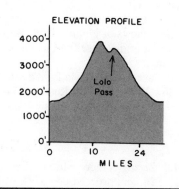

The foothills of Mount Hood offer few backroads suitable for bicycling. Since logging roads are not paved and the main highways are heavily trafficked, bicyclists usually visit the area only when it is necessary in order to cross the mountains on their way to central Oregon.

The upper reaches of the Sandy River Valley, however, offer an exceptional twenty-five-mile loop ride on paved roads, with relatively little traffic. Long, long hills and close-up views of Mount Hood all contribute to the alpine character of the ride.

Due to that alpine character, a few precautions should be taken. Carry an extra sweater or windbreaker, and maybe even a pair of warm gloves, in case the weather turns chilly. Make sure your legs are up to a relentless climb and your tires and brakes ready for a long, fast descent.

In late fall and early spring, a phone call to the Zigzag Ranger Station (224-5243) is advisable, not only to check on the weather, but also to determine if the roads are free of snow. In winter, the roads are normally not plowed to more than a few miles from U.S. Highway 26. The phone call is advisable any time of year if you plan to ride on a weekday trip because a portion of the ride may occasionally be closed to private vehicles due to heavy logging-truck traffic.

The ride starts in the community of Zigzag, at the Forest Service Ranger Station. After crossing U.S. Highway 26, the route follows Lolo Pass Road up the Sandy River for about four miles, then climbs to 3700 feet on a ridge known as Last Chance Mountain. Watch carefully for oncoming vehicles, as the road up the ridge is narrow and twisting. The ridge offers fine views of the valley of the Clear Fork of the Sandy River but, unfortunately, the valley has been marred by the construction of a major powerline and by extensive clearcutting.

From the ride's high point near mile 10.0, the road dips, then climbs slightly to Lolo Pass, where it rejoins Lolo Pass Road. The final leg of the ride is a 10.6-mile descent to Zigzag; 1500 feet of elevation are lost in the first six miles. The Lolo Pass Road is a full two lanes wide, but it has a bit of loose gravel on it in places and occasionally has a fair amount of traffic. Ride carefully.

If you're looking for a nice spot to lunch, two places come to mind. For superb views of Mount Hood, stop along the road near mile 10.0. Lower down, a bridge over the Clear Fork at mile 5.8 offers a pretty streamside setting.

If the ride up to Lolo Pass doesn't tire you out, an optional side trip can follow Forest Service Road 1825 east past McNeil and Lost Creek campgrounds toward the Romona Falls trail.

MILEAGE LOG

0.0 Zigzag Ranger Station. Leave the parking lot, carefully cross **U.S. 26**, and proceed one block west.

0.1 Turn right on **Lolo Pass Road**.

4.3 Bear right on **Forest Service Road 1825**, leaving Lolo Pass Road (F.S. Road 18).

5.0 Bear left on **Forest Service Road 1828**.

13.6 Lolo Pass. Elevation 3420. Turn left on **Lolo Pass Road** and follow it all the way to Zigzag. At mile 18.0, a dirt road on the left leads a few feet to a view of French's Dome, an unusual rock knob occasionally visited by rock climbers.

24.1 Zigzag. Carefully cross **U.S. 26**, turn left, and ride one block east.

24.2 Turn right into the parking lot at Zigzag Ranger Station. End of ride.

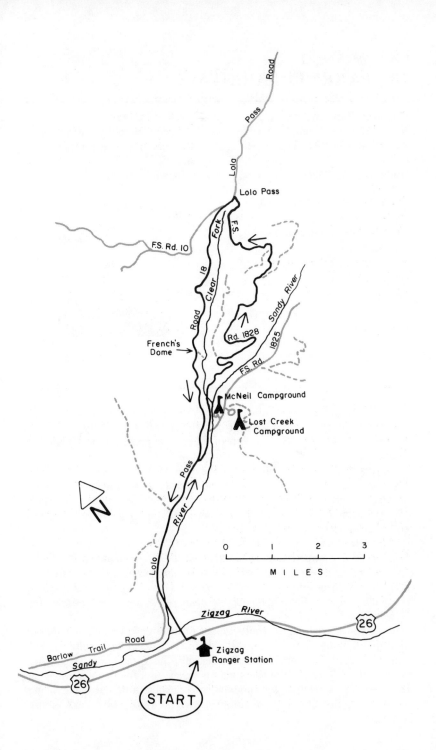

START

13 PARRETT MOUNTAIN

Starting Point: Wilsonville
Memorial Park, located 0.4 mile
east of I-5 exit 283 (Wilsonville
exit).
Distance: 39.7 miles.
Terrain: Hilly.
**Total Cumulative Elevation
Gain:** 2400 feet.
Recommended Time of Year:
Any season.
Recommended Starting Time:
Before 11:00 A.M.
Allow: 4 to 5 hours.

Points of Interest
Wilsonville Memorial Park
Parrett Mountain Greenway
  Access
Chehalem Mountains

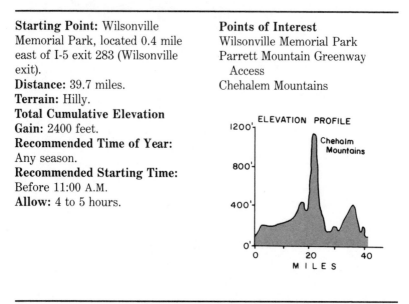

Parrett Mountain stands along the Willamette north of Champoeg State
Park, offering an expansive backdrop to the view from the bluffs overlook-
ing the park. At 1247 feet, it is one of the highest points in the Willamette
Valley.

Parrett Mountain also stands near the intersections of Clackamas, Yamhill, and Washington counties. This ride circles Parrett Mountain, visiting
all three counties. While the route keeps a safe distance from the steep hills
of Parrett Mountain itself, it does cross a 1125-foot pass at the southern
end of the nearby Chehalem Mountains.

The route starts at a large park just east of Wilsonville, then follows the
Willamette River upstream. The road along the river is quite varied, being
flat and sunny as it passes filbert orchards and pastures, then shady as it
occasionally drops into several small ravines. One of the prettiest roads in
the valley, it is a justifiably popular bike route for riders headed for
Newberg or French Prairie.

In the Newberg area, the route crosses State Highway 99W, then makes
an arduous climb up the southwest side of the Chehalem Mountains. The
climber is rewarded, first by views back into the Yamhill and Willamette
valleys, then by views into the Tualatin Valley, and finally by a sweeping
thousand-foot descent to the community of Scholls. A detour north, along
the crest of the Chehalem Mountains, to Bald Peak State Park is also
available.

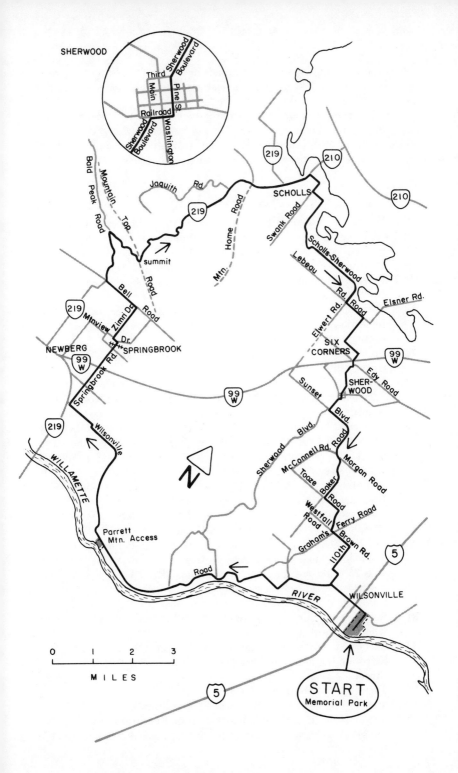

The route then follows flat farm roads along the Tualatin to Sherwood. Before returning to Wilsonville, the last leg of the ride passes through an area of rolling farmland known as Pleasant Hill.

For those seeking a longer ride, the route connects with several others described in this book, including Farmington-Scholls Loop (#6), Lower Tualatin Valley (#7), Chehalem Mountains (#19), and Three-Ferry Figure Eight (#44), while Petes Mountain (#14) lies just to the east.

MILEAGE LOG

0.0 Wilsonville Memorial Park. Ride north, toward the park entrance.

0.3 At the park entrance, turn left on **Wilsonville Road** and follow it under I-5 and through Wilsonville (store). Stay on Wilsonville Road as it follows the Willamette River west toward Newberg.

4.7 Parrett Mountain Access (day use only; no drinking water). A short trail leads to the Willamette River.

12.5 Turn right (north) on **Springbrook Road** a few feet before an intersection with Highway 219. At mile 13.6, cross Highway 99W and continue north on Springbrook Road.

14.5 Springbrook. After crossing the railroad tracks, bear left at an unmarked intersection (**Mountainview Drive**).

14.7 Turn right at an unmarked intersection (**Zimri Drive**).

15.6 Turn left at an unmarked T-intersection (**Bell Road** or **North Valley Road**).

16.6 Turn right at a T-intersection with **Highway 219**. (A left turn at mile 18.1 leads 5.4 miles to Bald Peak State Park.) The road climbs steadily up to a pass over the Chehalem Mountains at mile 19.7. The sign at the pass showing an elevation of 1272 feet refers to the knoll to the east; the pass is actually 1125 feet high. From the pass, follow Highway 219 down into the Tualatin Valley.

24.4 Scholls (store). Although Highway 219 turns left here, continue straight (northeast) on **Highway 210** (Scholls Ferry Road).

25.2 North Scholls (store). Turn right (east) on **Scholls-Sherwood Road** and follow it as it works its way south and east toward Sherwood. At mile 25.7, do not go straight on Swank Road but follow Scholls-Sherwood Road as it turns. Similar intersections occur at miles 29.4 and 29.9.

31.4 Six Corners (stores). Cross Highway 99W, then bear right on **Sherwood Boulevard**.

32.1 Sherwood. Sherwood Boulevard ends at an intersection with Pine Street on the left and Third Avenue on the right. Turn left on **Pine Street**.

32.2 Turn right on **Railroad Street**.

32.3 Turn left on **Sherwood Boulevard** (Main Street).

32.7 Turn left at an intersection with **Sunset Boulevard**. At mile 33.4, Sunset Boulevard curves right (south) and becomes **Baker Road**.

34.2 Follow Baker Road as it turns left at an intersection with McConnell Road.

34.3 Follow Baker Road as it turns right (south) at an intersection with Morgan Road.

35.3 Turn left on **Tooze Road**. At mile 35.8, the road turns south.

36.4 Bear left, following the arterial (**Brown Road**), at an intersection with Westfall Road. At mile 36.5, continue straight (east) through an intersection with Grahams Ferry Road (unmarked). At mile 36.9, the arterial turns right (south) and becomes **S.W. 110th Avenue**.

38.1 T-intersection with **Wilsonville Road**. Turn left, then use the bike lane on the south side of the road.

38.8 Wilsonville (store).

39.4 Entrance to Wilsonville Memorial Park. Turn right into the park.

39.7 Wilsonville Memorial Park. End of ride.

Clackamas County
14 PETES MOUNTAIN

Starting Point: Willamette Park, at the foot of 12th Street in the Willamette section of West Linn. Willamette is located two and a half miles south of West Linn on State Highway 212 or I-205.

Distance: 19.4 miles.

Terrain: Very hilly.

Total Cumulative Elevation Gain: 1750 feet.

Recommended Time of Year: Any season.

Recommended Starting Time: Before 1:00 P.M.

Allow: 2 to 3 hours.

Points of Interest
Willamette Park
Hebb Park

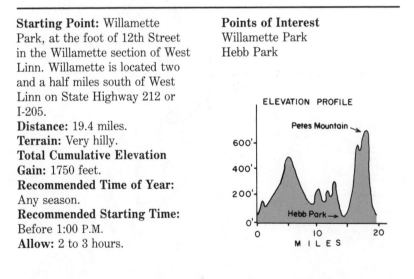

Between Canby and West Linn, the Willamette River makes a sharp bend as it turns around the foot of an eight-hundred-foot ridge known as Petes Mountain. Three roads meet near the summit of the ridge. The route described here climbs and descends the two steepest ones. Although it is a short ride and much of it traverses rolling farmland, it is not for those looking for a leisurely ride on flat farm roads.

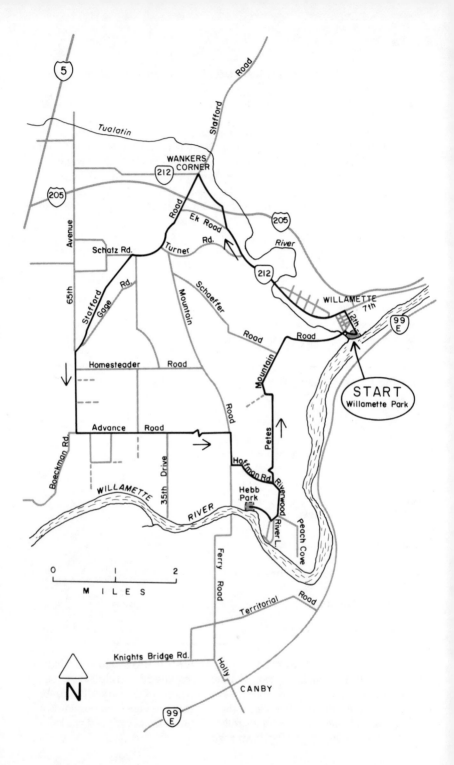

For some reason, several of the names shown on the road signs in this area conflict with those shown on most maps. The names used in this description are those found on the road signs. For riders using other maps, some of the alternate names are shown in parentheses in the mileage log.

In addition to some confusing road names, the route passes through several unusually named communities, or former communities, including Advance, Wankers Corner, Skunk Hollow, and Frog Pond. Perhaps as a result of their names, most of them no longer exist.

The route starts at the mouth of the Tualatin River, only fifty feet above sea level, and follows the Tualatin as it winds its way northwest to Wankers Corner. Following Stafford Road south, the route crosses the northern toe of Petes Mountain, then glides down through farmland (and spreading suburbia) toward Wilsonville.

Before reaching Wilsonville, the route turns east and, after a few miles of farmland, begins to climb over Petes Mountain. After gaining half of the ridge's eight hundred feet of elevation, the route drops back down to the Willamette River to visit Hebb Park, just upstream from the Canby Ferry.

The last two sections of the ride are the steepest. From Hebb Park, the route climbs from an elevation of 50 feet to 720 feet in only three and a half miles, with most of the elevation gained in the first mile and a half. The effort is rewarded on the last leg, when Petes Mountain Road drops back to the river in two miles that seem nearly vertical.

MILEAGE LOG

0.0 Willamette Park in the Willamette section of West Linn. Ride uphill (northwest) on **12th Street**, which is quite steep. Follow 12th Street as it joins **Tualatin Avenue** at mile 0.2 and a few blocks later enters "downtown" Willamette.

0.5 Turn left on **Highway 212** (7th Avenue). After leaving Willamette, 7th Avenue becomes **Borland Road**. At mile 1.8, the road crosses a bridge over the Tualatin River.

3.0 Follow Highway 212 (Borland Road) as it bears right at a Y-intersection with Ek Road (Barnes Road). The road passes under I-205 at mile 3.3.

4.0 Wankers Corner. Turn left on **Stafford Road**, cross I-205 on an overpass and follow Stafford Road south for several miles. At mile 5.9, follow Stafford Road as it bears left at an intersection with Schatz Road (Delker Road).

9.0 Turn left at a T-intersection with **Advance Road** (Boeckman Road). At mile 9.6, the road drops, with little warning, into a small, but very steep, ravine. In addition to being steep, the road is fairly rough and not at all suitable for breakneck speeds, so ride carefully. Another such ravine occurs at mile 10.9.

11.7 T-intersection with **Mountain Road**. Turn right.

12.2 Turn left on **Hoffman Road**.

13.0 Turn right on **Riverwood Drive**.

13.6 At a Y-intersection with Peach Cove Road, bear right, following signs to Hebb Park.

13.7 Bear right at a Y-intersection with River Lane on the left.

13.8 At another Y-intersection, bear right on **Hebb Park Road**.

14.3 Hebb Park. After lunch or a break, follow the route back to **Hoffman Road**.

15.6 Intersection of Riverwood Drive, Hoffman Road, and Petes Mountain Road. Turn right on **Petes Mountain Road**, which climbs steeply over the shoulder of Petes Mountain, then drops into the community of Willamette.

19.3 Immediately after crossing the Tualatin River, turn right on **14th Street**.

19.4 Willamette Park. End of ride.

Clackamas County

15 CLACKAMAS RIVER

Starting Point: Barton Park. From Milwaukie, follow State Highway 224 east 15 miles to Barton, then turn south.

Distance: 44.0 miles.

Terrain: Very hilly.

Total Cumulative Elevation Gain: 2900 feet.

Recommended Time of Year: Any season.

Recommended Starting Time: 10:00 A.M.

Allow: 5 hours.

Points of Interest

Barton Park

Metzler Park

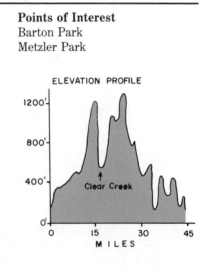

Bicycling near the Clackamas River is similar to riding along the Sandy River to the north. Both rivers have cut deep valleys into the western foothills of the Cascades, leaving steep wooded hills interspersed with high plateaus of farmland. The Clackamas Valley is not as deep as the Sandy River Gorge, so the riding is not as strenuous, but the Clackamas area is definitely hilly. This is a fine ride for those looking for a good workout over varied terrain.

The work getting to the top of the hills will be rewarded with great views of Mount Hood, visits to small farming communities, and long, twisting descents on shady mountain roads. A few of the roads, however, have some moderate traffic; inexperienced riders may want to try a lonelier ride.

The route described is a 44.0-mile loop through the communities of Barton, Estacada, and Beaver Creek. The hills will make some of those 45 miles seem very long indeed. For riders who prefer a shorter trip, a shortcut can be used to reduce the total length to 36.8 miles; the shortcut also eliminates a few of the hills.

The route begins near Barton, at a large county park on the Clackamas, then follows the river upstream to Estacada. From Estacada, the route strikes out for the hills and plateaus southwest of the river. In the first four miles after leaving Estacada, the route gains 750 feet of elevation, then drops into the Clear Creek Valley. The highest elevation is reached a few miles later, near the community of Highland, when the route crosses the shoulder of Highland Butte at mile 23.

The route includes few parks, but one a few miles off the route is worth a

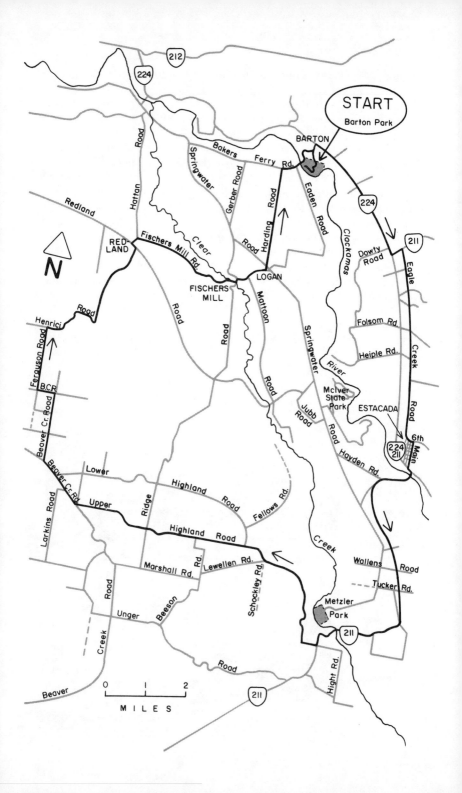

visit. Metzler Park, located along a secluded stretch of Clear Creek, near the southernmost point of the ride, makes a fine lunch stop. If the hills on the route tire you out, however, don't visit Metzler Park. Although the park is only 2.6 miles from the route, it is at the bottom of a five-hundred-foot hill that must be climbed to return to the route.

If you find you enjoy tackling the hills of the Clackamas River area, you should also try Trip #17, McIver-Molalla, which is nearly the same length as this ride but hillier. The two routes cross paths at two or three points and can be combined to truly test your hill-climbing fortitude.

MILEAGE LOG

0.0 Barton Park, at the parking lot near the boat ramp. Ride toward the park entrance, which is passed at mile 0.9.

1.0 Continue north on **Bakers Ferry Road**, rather than turning left toward the Barton Bridge.

1.2 Barton (store). Turn right at a T-intersection with **Highway 224**.

4.6 Turn left on **Highway 211**.

4.8 Turn right on an unmarked road (**Eagle Creek Road**). Pass through the community of Currinsville (store) at mile 7.9. At mile 9.6, the road curves left and becomes **Sixth Avenue** in Estacada.

9.7 Turn right on **Main Street**.

10.4 Turn left at a T-intersection with **Highway 224** (which is also Highway 211). Be careful on this busy road.

10.5 Turn right on **Highway 211**, then cross a bridge over the Clackamas River. Follow Highway 211 for 7 miles, up over a 1200-foot ridge, then down into the Clear Creek Valley and up the other side. (To visit Metzler Park, turn right on Tucker Road at mile 14.5, then turn left on Metzler Park Road 0.6 mile later.)

17.8 Turn right on **Highland Road** (Upper Highland Road) and follow it up onto a plateau, then down into the Beaver Creek Valley. (A short-cut, which shortens the ride by 8.7 miles, is available at mile 24.3 by turning north on Ridge Road and following it to Fischers Mill, which is at mile 40.1 on the regular route.)

26.2 Turn right at a T-intersection with **Beaver Creek Road**. Follow Beaver Creek Road north, then west when it turns left at mile 29.3.

29.9 Turn right on **Ferguson Road** (Meyrick or Danny Road).

31.4 Turn right on **Henrici Road**. At mile 31.7, the road turns north and begins to drop steeply to Abernethy Creek. The road eventually climbs back up to the Redland area.

35.3 Turn left on **Redland Road**.

35.4 Redland (store). Turn right on **Fischers Mill Road**. At mile 35.6, bear right on Fischers Mill Road at an intersection with Hattan Road. A few miles later, the road descends into the Clear Creek Valley.

38.6 Fischers Mill. Turn left, following Fischers Mill Road.

39.5 Logan. Bear left when the road forks, then cross Springwater Road and ride north on **Harding Road**.

41.9 Turn right at a T-intersection with **Bakers Ferry Road**. At mile 42.5, the road crosses a bridge over the Clackamas River.

43.1 When the road curves left, turn right toward Barton Park.

44.0 Barton Park parking lot. End of ride.

Clackamas County

16 RIPPLEBROOK

Starting Point: Estacada City Hall, at the corner of 5th Avenue and Main Street in Estacada (one block north of State Highway 224 on Main Street).
Distance: 54.6 miles.
Terrain: Moderate.
Total Cumulative Elevation Gain: 1100 feet.
Recommended Time of Year: Any season except mid-winter.
Recommended Starting Time: 9:00 A.M.
Allow: 6 hours.

Points of Interest
Clackamas River
Cazadero Dam
North Fork Dam
Numerous parks and camp-
  grounds

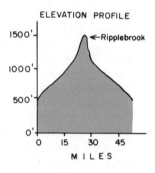

Ripplebrook could hardly be a more descriptive name. The shade from the evergreens is mixed with a patchwork of sunlight that filters through the forest. A few feet away, a stream gurgles as it flows along its bed of mossy boulders. Located on the Oak Grove Fork of the Clackamas River, this idyllic spot is just 27 miles southeast of Estacada.

The route described here starts in Estacada, follows the Clackamas River for those 27 miles, then returns to Estacada via the same route. Although the road is uphill nearly all the way to Ripplebrook, the grade is fairly gentle. The ride does have one drawback, however. The road (State Highway 224) is well used in summer by cars and campers headed for the camp-

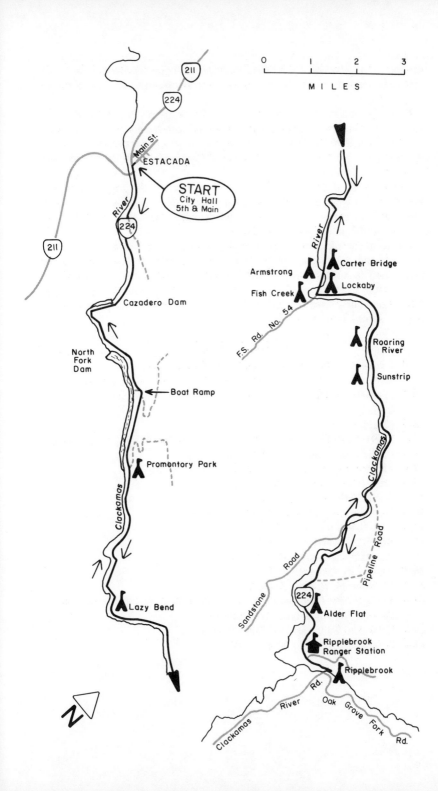

grounds that line the route. Especially on summer weekends, the route should be ridden only by those familiar with the hazards of narrow mountain roads.

An off-season ride may be the answer for those not willing to risk the summer conditions. Although Ripplebrook is located deep in the Cascades, it is less than 1500 feet in elevation, and thus in some years receives little or no snow. For current road conditions, call the Ripplebrook Ranger Station at 630-4256.

Although the upper part of the route is very woodsy and remote, the lower section is hardly wilderness, since the flow of the Clackamas River has been interrupted by two large hydroelectric dams, Cazadero Dam at mile 3.5 and North Fork Dam at mile 4.8.

The Ripplebrook area can be used as a lay-over point for a longer excursion into the mountains. From Ripplebrook, paved roads continue south along the Clackamas and Collawash rivers and east along the Oak Grove Fork of the Clackamas. The large number of campgrounds makes overnight rides fairly easy to plan, and several hot springs in the area can be used to soothe tired muscles.

MILEAGE LOG

0.0 Estacada City Hall. Ride south on **Main Street**.

0.1 Turn left (southeast) on **Highway 224** (Clackamas Highway).

0.4 Continue straight on Highway 224 when Highway 211 turns south (right).

3.5 Cazadero Dam.

4.8 North Fork Dam and overlook area. Note the fish ladder below.

6.2 Public boat ramp and day use area.

7.6 Promontory Park campground and day use area.

11.0 Lazy Bend Campground.

15.5 Carter Bridge Campground.

16.0 Lockaby and Armstrong campgrounds.

16.2 Fish Creek Campground.

18.8 Roaring River Campground.

19.3 Sunstrip Campground.

26.4 Alder Flat Campground.

26.7 Ripplebrook Ranger Station.

27.3 Ripplebrook Campground, the turn-around point of the route. Retrace the route back to Estacada.

54.5 Estacada. Turn right on **Main Street**.

54.6 Estacada City Hall. End of ride.

17 McIVER-MOLALLA

Starting Point: Milo McIver
State Park west of Estacada on
the Clackamas River. Park at the
McIver Memorial Viewpoint.
Distance: 42.8 miles.
Terrain: Very hilly.
**Total Cumulative Elevation
Gain:** 3600 feet.
Recommended Time of Year:
Any season.
Recommended Starting Time:
Before 10:00 A.M.
Allow: 5 hours.

Points of Interest
Milo McIver State Park
Metzler Park
Feyrer Park

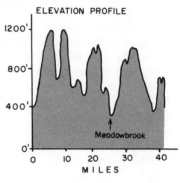

This ride crosses from the upper Clackamas River to the upper Molalla
River and in the process climbs up and down several intervening ridges. It
then turns around and follows a hilly route back again.

The hills are numerous and long, but the scenery is superb. Strong riders
will have no difficulty, and less ambitious riders shouldn't be frightened off.
With an early start, a slow but steady pace, and an occasional rest along the
way, most riders will find the ride to their liking.

Two parks along the route make fine rest stops, but since both are
located off the main loop, and at the bottom of hills that must be reclimbed
after visiting the parks, they are described as optional detours. The first,
Metzler Park, involves a five-hundred-foot drop into the Clear Creek Valley,
while the second, Feyrer Park, requires a three-hundred-foot descent to the
Molalla River. Both parks are worth a visit if the legs are willing.

If the legs are less than willing, the mileage log describes two shortcuts
that can be used to reduce the ride by up to 15 miles. Since Trip #15 covers
some of the same territory and crosses paths with this route at two or three
places, it can also be used to shorten or expand the loop described here.

The ride starts at Milo McIver State Park along the Clackamas River.
During the summer, the park is used heavily by kayakers, rafters, and pic-
nickers. On warm weekends, traffic near the park is moderately heavy but
thins out just a few miles away. Also during the summer, a small admission
charge is collected; carry your ticket with you on your bike for free re-
admission to the park.

Riders driving from the Salem area may prefer to start the route at its southern end by parking at Feyrer Park, three miles east of Molalla.

MILEAGE LOG

0.0 Milo McIver Memorial Viewpoint in Milo McIver State Park. Ride out of the viewpoint parking lot, then turn right and follow the road to the park entrance.

0.7 Turn left at a T-intersection with **Springwater Road** and follow it south for five miles. At mile 4.9, the road passes through the hamlet of Springwater. At mile 5.5, follow Springwater Road as it turns 90 degrees left (east). (To make a side trip to Metzler Park—drinking water available; overnight camping permitted—continue south on Metzler Park Road for two miles.)

6.0 A few feet before an intersection with Highway 211, follow Springwater Road when it turns right (south) and parallels Highway 211.

6.9 Continue south on **Highway 211** when Springwater Road joins it. Highway 211 drops into the Clear Creek Valley, then climbs over a ridge to the town of Colton at mile 14.7. (For a shortcut that decreases the route by 14.8 miles, turn right on Unger Road at mile 10.6. After another 5.3 miles, Unger Road reaches the community of Clarkes, which is located at mile 30.7 of the regular route.)

16.2 Turn left on **Dhooghe Road**. (Another shortcut is available by staying on Highway 211 for approximately three miles; it will rejoin the regular route at mile 26.0, thus shortening the route by about seven miles.)

19.7 Dhooghe Road curves to the west and becomes **Fernwood Road**.

22.7 Turn right (north) at a T-intersection with **Wright Road**. (At mile 23.5, a side trip to Feyrer Park on the Molalla River—day use only; drinking water available—can be made by turning left on Feyrer Park Road. One-half mile after leaving Wright Road, turn right over a bridge, then turn right into the park.)

25.3 Turn right at a T-intersection with **Highway 211**.

26.0 Meadowbrook (store). Continue straight (northeast) on **Beaver Creek Road** when Highway 211 turns right.

32.0 Turn right on **Butte Road** (store).

32.7 Turn left (north) on **Ridge Road**. The road follows the crest of a ridge known as the Hogback, then drops into the Clear Creek Valley.

38.2 Turn right on **Redland Road**, which continues to drop toward Clear Creek. At mile 40.9, follow Redland Road when it turns left at an intersection with Jubb Road.

41.4 Turn right at a T-intersection with **Springwater Road**.

42.1 Turn left into Milo McIver State Park and follow the signs to the Memorial Viewpoint.

42.8 Milo McIver Memorial Viewpoint. End of ride.

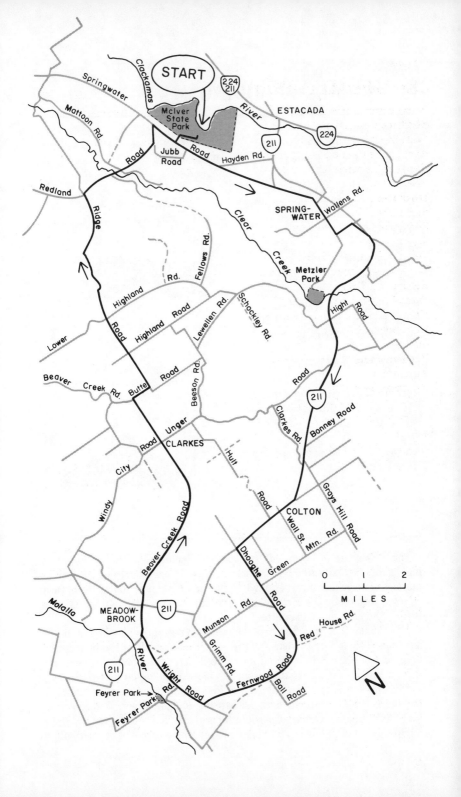

18 MOLALLA-PUDDING

Starting Point: Molalla River State Park, north of Canby just west of the Canby Ferry landing. Canby is 20 miles south of Portland on State Highway 99E.

Distance: Pudding River loop— 29.6 miles. Molalla River loop— 38.9 miles. Combined loop— 49.4 miles.

Terrain: Pudding River loop—rolling farmland. Molalla River loop—flat with a few hills.

Total Cumulative Elevation Gain: Pudding River loop—650 feet. Molalla River loop—950 feet.

Recommended Time of Year: Any season.

Recommended Starting Time: Before noon for either loop; before 10:00 A.M. for a combined loop.

Allow: 3 to 4 hours; 5 hours for a combined loop.

Points of Interest
Molalla River State Park
Feyrer Park
Wagon Wheel Park

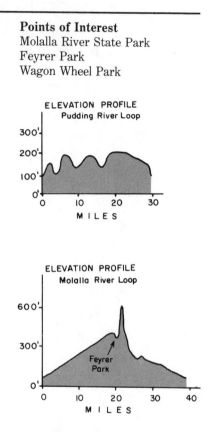

The area south of Canby offers classic Willamette Valley bicycling: rolling farms, meandering rivers, dozens of level backroads, and an infinite number of possible routes. The two routes described here follow the natural triangle formed by the Molalla and Pudding rivers, which join near Canby before entering the Willamette.

The Molalla River is a fast-moving mountain stream, while the Pudding is a farmland slough that twists and turns on its slow route to Canby from the area east of Salem. It received its name, not from its murky waters, but from a group of pioneers that made elk-blood pudding on its banks.

The Pudding River loop follows the Pudding southwest from Canby. At Hubbard, the route turns east toward the Molalla River, a dozen miles away. After only six miles, the route turns north and returns to Canby, for a trip total of 29.6 miles. The Molalla River loop completes the crossing to the Molalla, visits two parks, then returns to Canby via the north bank of the river.

Either loop provides a pleasant three or four hours of bicycling. The two loops can also be combined into one 49.4-mile loop by eliminating the north-south leg that they share. The resulting ride follows the full triangle from Canby to Hubbard to Molalla and back to Canby. Even longer routes are possible, since several backroads lead west to Champoeg, south to Mount Angel, or east to Estacada.

MILEAGE LOG

PUDDING RIVER LOOP

0.0 Molalla River State Park (day use only; drinking water available). Ride east toward the park entrance.

0.1 Bear right at the park entrance.

0.2 Turn right at a T-intersection with **Ferry Road** (unmarked).

2.2 Turn right on **Knights Bridge Road** near a small city park. The road crosses Knights Bridge over the Molalla River at mile 2.9, then turns south at mile 4.1.

4.5 Turn right at a T-intersection with **Arndt Road**, then cross a bridge over the Pudding River. Arndt Road crosses Airport Road at mile 6.1 and Hubbard Highway at mile 6.4.

6.9 Turn left (south) on **Stoller Road**, which soon becomes **Boones Ferry Road**.

9.0 Boones Ferry Road eventually parallels Hubbard Highway, then reaches a T-intersection with **Ehlen Road** (Fargo Road). Turn right, then immediately turn left (south) on **Boones Ferry Road**.

9.7 Bear left, following Boones Ferry Road, at an intersection with Donald Road.

12.4 Turn left on **Mineral Springs Road**, which becomes **D Street** in Hubbard. A city park is located at mile 13.3 between 4th and 5th streets. Cross Highway 99E at mile 13.5.

13.7 Turn right on **Oak Street**.

13.8 Turn left at a T-intersection with **Whiskey Hill Road** (J Street). Follow Whiskey Hill Road east for several miles, crossing the Pudding River at mile 16.3. Pass through the community of Whiskey Hill (store) at mile 16.7, where Whiskey Hill Road becomes **Barnards Road**.

20.2 Turn left (north) on **Canby-Marquam Road**. (This intersection is mile 9.5 of the Molalla River loop. Continue east from this intersection to ride the 49.4-mile perimeter of both loops.) When Canby-Marquam Road enters Canby, it becomes **Ivy Street**.

26.8 Canby. Cross Highway 99E.

26.9 Turn left on **1st Avenue**.

26.8 Turn right (north) on **Holly Street**, which becomes **Ferry Road** after passing through an intersection with Knights Bridge Road at mile 27.2.

29.4 Turn left at a sign pointing to Molalla River State Park.

29.6 Molalla River State Park. End of ride.

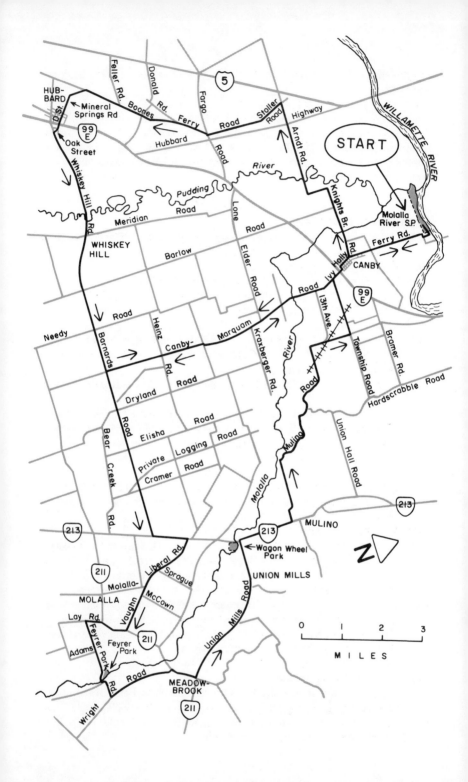

MOLALLA RIVER LOOP

0.0 Molalla River State Park. Ride east toward the park entrance.

0.1 Bear right at the park entrance.

0.2 Turn right at a T-intersection with **Ferry Road**, which eventually becomes **Holly Street** in Canby.

2.6 Turn left on **1st Avenue**.

2.7 Turn right (south) on **Ivy Street**, cross Highway 99E, then follow Ivy Street south for seven miles. After leaving Canby, Ivy Street becomes **Canby-Marquam Road**.

9.5 Turn left on **Barnards Road** and follow it east for four miles.

13.7 Turn left at a T-intersection with **Highway 213**.

14.6 Turn right on an unmarked road with a tavern on the corner (**Molalla-Liberal Road**). (For a shortcut, continue north on Highway 213 for 1.4 miles, where mile 27.2 of the regular route rejoins Highway 213.)

16.1 When Molalla-Liberal Road curves to the right and becomes Molalla Avenue, bear left on **Vaughn Road**.

17.4 Turn right (south) at a T-intersection with **Highway 211**.

18.2 Turn left on a road (**Lay Road**) marked by a sign pointing to Feyrer Park (store).

18.5 Follow the arterial by turning left on **Feyrer Park Road** (Dickie Prairie Road or Robbins Road).

20.1 Feyrer Park (day use only; drinking water available).

20.2 Immediately after crossing a bridge over the Molalla River, turn left at a T-intersection, following Feyrer Park Road.

20.7 Turn left at a T-intersection with **Wright Road**.

22.5 Turn right at a T-intersection with **Highway 211**.

23.2 Meadowbrook (store). Turn left on **Union Mills Road**. At mile 25.9, pass through the community of Union Mills (store).

27.2 Turn right (north) at a T-intersection with **Highway 213**. Ride carefully on this road; it has no shoulders. (A left turn here, then another left turn immediately after crossing a bridge, will take the rider to Wagon Wheel Park, an undeveloped county park on the Molalla River.)

28.6 Mulino (store). Turn left on **Mulino Road** and follow it north and west for six miles.

34.1 Follow Mulino Road north, under a railroad trestle, when 13th Avenue (Mundorf Road) curves to the left.

34.7 Turn left on **Township Road**.

36.0 Turn right at a T-intersection with **Ivy Street**, then cross Highway 99E.

36.2 Turn left on **1st Avenue**.

36.3 Turn right on **Holly Street**, which becomes **Ferry Road** at an intersection with Knights Bridge Road at mile 36.7.

38.7 Turn left at a sign pointing to Molalla River State Park.

38.9 Molalla River State Park. End of ride.

19 CHEHALEM MOUNTAINS

Starting Point: Herbert Hoover Memorial Park in Newberg, one block south of State Highway 99W on River Street.
Distance: 51.7 miles (31.5 miles if a shortcut is used).
Terrain: Extremely steep hills and moderately flat farmland.
Total Cumulative Elevation Gain: 2800 feet.
Recommended Time of Year: Any season.
Recommended Starting Time: 9:00 A.M.
Allow: 6 hours.
Points of Interest
Herbert Hoover Memorial Park
Minthorn House
Laurelwood Academy
Bald Peak State Park

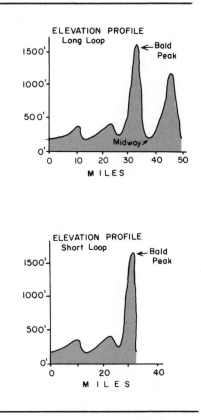

The Chehalem Mountains form a 13-mile-long dorsal fin running from Forest Grove southeast to Newberg, dividing the Tualatin and Yamhill valleys. This strenuous trip crosses the Chehalem Mountains, not once, but twice, and visits their highest point, Bald Peak State Park. Be prepared for long hills, probably steeper than any you've seen before, but expect rewarding views in return.

The trip starts in Newberg at a park named for Herbert Hoover, just across the street from the house he lived in as a child. The house is open to the public for a small admission fee.

From Newberg, the route follows State Highway 240 west through the Yamhill Valley farmland once held by Ewing Young, an Oregon pioneer and reputed horse thief. When Young died in 1841 without known heirs, his neighbors elected Oregon's first judge to decide who would inherit Young's property. The judge probated Young's estate under the laws of New York,

"Thanks, kid!"

since Oregon had no probate statutes of its own. This provisional government used the proceeds of the Young estate to build Oregon's first jail but later, when Young's son was located, the funds were returned to him. Today, Young is said to lie under a huge oak near Highway 240.

Small towns dot this ride. Carlton and Yamhill, typical of small Willamette Valley farming communities, have yet to be disturbed by freeways and suburbs. Old churches, grain elevators, cemeteries, and grange halls have thus been spared the bulldozer's wrath.

Laurelwood, on the other hand, is far from typical. Nestled at the very foot of the Chehalem Mountains, Laurelwood consists of a secluded Seventh Day Adventist boarding school and not much else.

From Laurelwood, the road climbs abruptly to the 1629-foot summit of Bald Peak. Few roads in Oregon are as steep, but fortunately the route is well shaded and free of much auto traffic.

From Bald Peak, the route drops quickly to the Tualatin Valley, then passes through such one-building towns as Laurel, Midway, and Scholls. From Scholls, the route climbs over the southern end of the Chehalem Mountains to return to the Yamhill Valley.

The length of the ride can be shortened, and one of the long climbs eliminated, by continuing south after visiting Bald Peak State Park. After dropping down a 5.4-mile hill from the park, the road rejoins the regular route at mile 47.5, reducing the length of the ride by 20.2 miles.

MILEAGE LOG

0.0 Herbert Hoover Memorial Park, at the corner of River Street and Second Avenue in Newberg. On the northwest corner is the Minthorn House (1881), boyhood home of Herbert Hoover. Proceed west on **Second Avenue**.

0.5 Turn right on **Main Street**. Proceed north, crossing Highway 99W at mile 0.6, where Main Street becomes **Highway 240**. Follow Highway 240 as it turns west at mile 0.9 and leaves Newberg. On the right at mile 4.3 is the Ewing Young historical marker. At mile 5.9, where County Road 101 intersects Highway 240, stands tiny Valley View School (ca. 1909), long since abandoned.

6.5 Turn left on **Marr Road**.

8.3 Bear right (west) on **Carlton-Newberg Road** (unmarked), which eventually becomes **Main Street** in Carlton.

12.1 Carlton. Continue straight through the town. On the far side of town, Main Street becomes **Meadowlake Road**.

13.5 Turn right on **West Side Road**.

16.7 Intersection with Moores Valley Road. Continue straight on **Moores Valley Road**. At mile 16.8, cross a bridge over the North Yamhill River.

16.9 Turn right, staying on Moores Valley Road.

18.5 Yamhill. Moores Valley Road has become **Main Street**. Turn left on **Maple Street** (Highway 47) and follow it as it turns east a few blocks north of Main Street. At mile 19.2, the road turns north again.

24.1 Turn right on **Wapato-Newberg Road** (unmarked).

25.6 At a T-intersection, turn left on **Spring Hill Road** (unmarked).

27.3 Turn right on **Laurelwood Road**. Follow this road as it works its way east and north to the town of Laurelwood at mile 28.8, home of Laurelwood Academy, a Seventh Day Adventist boarding high school. Immediately after leaving Laurelwood, the road climbs up the steep west side of the Chehalem Mountains.

30.6 Turn right at a T-intersection with **Bald Peak Road**.

32.6 Turn right into Bald Peak State Park (day use area only; no drinking water). Elevation 1629 feet.

32.7 Return to **Bald Peak Road** and turn left (north). (For a shortcut, continue south on Bald Peak Road for 5.4 miles; here the road rejoins the regular route at mile 47.5.)

34.6 At the intersection with Laurelwood Road, bear right, staying on Bald Peak Road.

35.8 Bald Peak Road bears left here. Ride straight on **Laurel Road West** (unmarked) down a very steep hill. Notwithstanding a Rough Road sign, the road was recently repaved and is relatively smooth.

37.5 Laurel, a town that consists solely of the Laurel Valley Store. Ride straight (east) on **Laurel Road East**.

39.0 T-intersection with Highway 219. Turn right, following **Highway 219** through the town of Midway (a tavern) to Scholls.

41.3 Intersection of Highways 219 and 210 at Scholls (store). Turn right (south), following Highway 219 as it climbs up over the southern end of the Chehalem Mountains.

46.1 Yamhill County line and the summit of the pass over the Chehalem

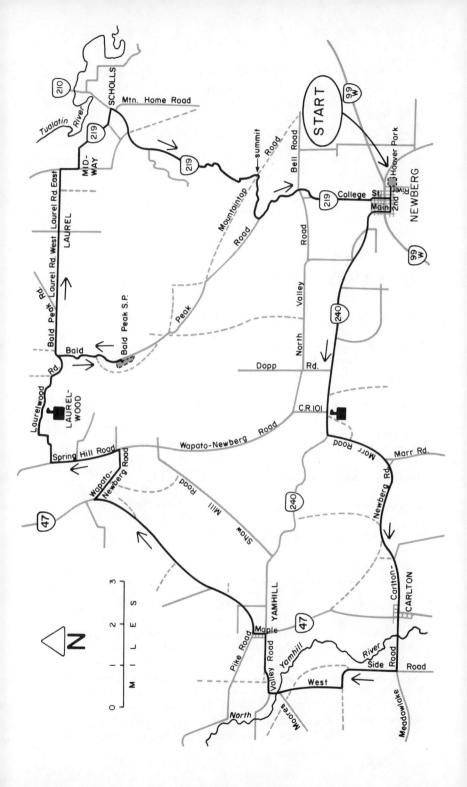

Mountains. The sign showing an elevation of 1272 feet refers to the knoll to the east; the height of the pass is actually 1125 feet. The road proceeds down a long, steep hill to Newberg, where it becomes **College Street**.

50.9   Bear left, following Highway 219 and College Street.
51.5   Turn left on **Second Avenue**.
51.7   Hoover Park, at the corner of Second Avenue and River Street. End of ride.

Yamhill County
20 LAFAYETTE

Starting Point: Yamhill County Historical Society Museum, at the corner of Sixth and Market streets in Lafayette, 30 miles west of Portland on State Highway 99W. From Highway 99W in Lafayette, drive three blocks north on Market Street.
Distance: 30.0 miles.
Terrain: Flat with some gentle hills.
Total Cumulative Elevation Gain: 675 feet.
Recommended Time of Year: Any season.
Recommended Starting Time: Before noon.
Allow: 3½ **hours.**

Points of Interest
Yamhill County Historical
  Society Museum
Our Lady of Guadalupe Trappist
  Abbey

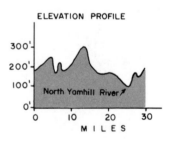

This pretty ride explores the rolling foothills and farmland north of Lafayette, including the Chehalem Valley and the valley of the North Yamhill River. While the route is not notable for unusual vistas or spacious parks, it can be highly recommended as a varied, low-traffic tour for a relaxing day in the country.

The route starts in Lafayette, a small cluster of buildings on State Highway 99W. Almost a century and a half ago, Lafayette was one of the primary commercial centers of the territory, shipping a large volume of farm products to the California gold fields via pack trains. But due to the falls on the Yamhill River just downstream from the town, Lafayette was a

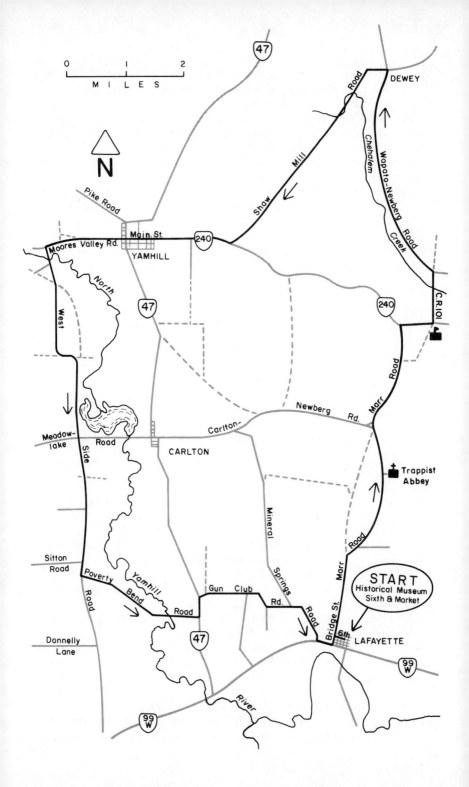

poor river port. By the time locks were built on the river in 1900, the railroads had usurped much of the shipping business, and Lafayette's commercial importance never recovered.

Before the turn of the century, Lafayette was the home of a successful seminary. Today, a Trappist abbey makes its home in the hills a few miles north of town. A relatively reclusive order, the Trappist monks historically took vows of silence. The vows are no longer taken, and visitors are welcome to tour their modest abbey and book bindery.

The route starts in Lafayette at an 1892 church now being used as a county historical museum. After leaving the small town, the ride climbs a subtle grade through woodlands and small farms past the Trappist abbey, then drops gently down into the Chehalem Creek Valley. The narrow, sparsely populated valley seems isolated; the single road through it runs neither to nor from anyplace in particular, and the few residents seem to live unhurried lives.

From the north end of the Chehalem Valley, the route climbs over a low pass and coasts past farms and dairies on its way to the town of Yamhill. The remainder of the ride is mostly flat, generally following the North Yamhill River as it winds its way south toward Lafayette.

MILEAGE LOG

0.0 Yamhill County Historical Society Museum in Lafayette. Ride three blocks west on **Sixth Street**.

0.1 Turn right on **Bridge Street** and follow it as it becomes **Marr Road** and proceeds through the foothills and farmland north of town. Our Lady of Guadalupe Trappist Abbey is on the right at mile 2.9. At mile 4.0, bear right, staying on Marr Road.

5.8 T-intersection with **Highway 240**. Turn right.

6.4 Turn left (north) on **County Road 101**. Valley View School, a ca. 1909 one-room schoolhouse, stands abandoned on the south side of this intersection.

7.2 Bear left on **Wapato-Newberg Road** (unmarked) at an intersection with North Valley Road and Ribbon Ridge Road.

11.0 This intersection is labelled on most maps as the community of Dewey, but no buildings are in evidence. Turn left on **Shaw Mill Road** (unmarked) and follow it west, then southwest.

15.2 T-intersection with **Highway 240**. Turn right and follow it into Yamhill, where it becomes **Main Street**.

17.1 Intersection with Highway 47 in "downtown" Yamhill. Continue straight (west). After leaving Yamhill, Main Street becomes **Moores Valley Road**.

18.6 Turn left, following Moores Valley Road (unmarked). At mile 18.7, cross the North Yamhill River on a concrete bridge.

18.8 Moores Valley Road turns right. Ride straight (south) on **West Side Road** (unmarked). At mile 22.1, go straight through an intersection with Meadowlake Road.

24.4 Turn left on **Poverty Bend Road** (unmarked). This road is the only paved left turn in the vicinity; it can also be recognized by a 20-ton load limit sign. The load limit sign will be more fully understood at mile 26.1, where a narrow wooden plank bridge crosses the North Yamhill River.

26.6 T-intersection with **Highway 47**. Turn left.

26.9 Turn right on an unmarked road (**Gun Club Road**) and follow it east toward Lafayette. It eventually joins Mineral Springs Road at mile 28.6.

29.4 T-intersection with **Highway 99W**. Carefully cross the highway, then turn left, using the shoulder.

29.7 Turn left on **Bridge Street**, which is the second street on the left after entering Lafayette.

29.8 Turn right on **Sixth Street**.

30.0 Corner of Sixth and Market streets. End of ride.

Yamhill County
21 GRAND ISLAND

Starting Point: City Park in Dayton, 30 miles west of Portland just south of State Highways 99W and 18. Park on the east side of the park, near the corner of Third and Ferry streets.

Distance: 36.3 miles.

Terrain: Flat with one moderately long hill.

Total Cumulative Elevation Gain: 550 feet.

Recommended Time of Year: Any season

Recommended Starting Time: Before 11:00 A.M.

Allow: 4 hours.

Points of Interest
Historic buildings in Dayton
Grand Island
Maude Williamson State Park

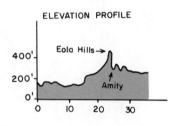

Grand Island lies in the Willamette River about 60 rivermiles upstream from Portland, in the heart of a rich agricultural area. With the exception of Sauvie Island, it appears to be the largest island in the Willamette. The

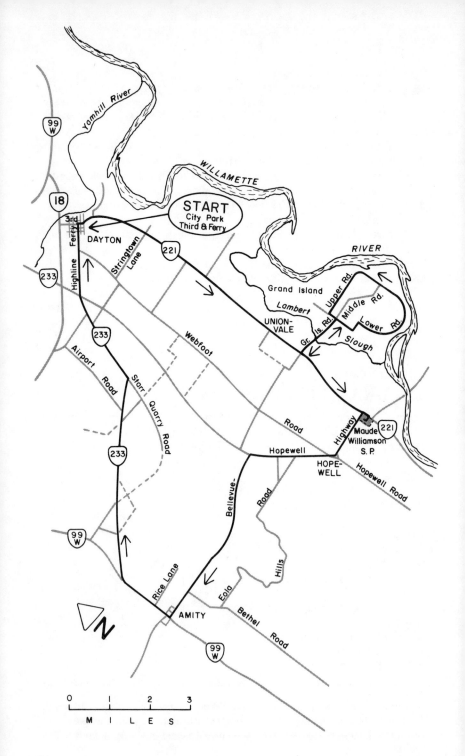

route described here circles Grand Island and visits several of the nearby farming communities.

The ride starts in Dayton, a small town with a history typical of Willamette Valley towns. Founded as a mill town, Dayton's Yamhill River waterfront was first visited by sternwheelers in 1851. By serving the shipping needs of area farmers, the town prospered and quickly expanded around its large central square. Fluctuating water levels, however, made the river an undependable carrier of freight, and the growth of the town slowed after railroads and highways proved superior to the river and its steamers.

Being bypassed, however, by both the railroad and State Highway 99W had certain advantages. Dayton has a surprising concentration of historic buildings that might not have survived had the town continued to grow. After your ride, pedal your bike around Dayton's shaded streets and admire some of the buildings, particularly the churches, which have survived from the last century.

From Dayton's central square, the ride proceeds south through flat farmland for several miles, then turns east to Grand Island. The island is separated from the mainland by the Lambert Slough, a brush- and weed-choked channel of the Willamette. A narrow farm road circles the southern end of the flat island, which is only a few feet higher than the river itself.

In late summer and fall, the island's farmers operate several fruit and vegetable stands to market their produce. The prices are low and the produce fresh. If you are planning a fall ride, count on buying some or all of your lunch at the fruit stands, then bicycling a few miles south to picnic at Maude Williamson State Park. The park consists of a large grove of evergreens, which seems out of place in the surrounding flat farmland.

From the state park the ride proceeds west to Hopewell, a very small town clustered around an interesting church (ca. 1880) and a schoolhouse built near the turn of the century. From Hopewell, the route turns north and east to eventually cross the Eola Hills. The climb over the hills, which is about a mile and a half long, ends with a rapid descent to the town of Amity. From Amity, the ride turns north, then skirts the north end of the Eola Hills on its way northeast to Dayton.

MILEAGE LOG

0.0 City Park in Dayton. From the east side of the park, ride south on **Third Street (Highway 221)**. Follow this road for several miles as it travels through the farmland south of Dayton. At mile 5.7, the road passes through the community of Unionvale.

6.7 Grand Island Junction (store). Turn left on **Grand Island Road**. At mile 7.2, cross Lambert Slough onto Grand Island.

8.0 This intersection, known as Four Corners, is the junction of Upper, Lower, and Middle Island roads. (The north end of the island is apparently considered the upper end, even though it is the downstream end of the island.) Turn right on **Lower Island Road** and follow it around the perimeter of the island. At mile 11.4, do not turn left on Middle Island Road, but continue north from Lower Island Road onto **Upper Island Road**.

13.2 T-intersection. Turn left.

13.4 Four Corners. Turn right (west) and return to the mainland.

14.7 Grand Island Junction (store). Turn left on **Highway 221**. At mile 16.7, go straight, past a road on the right (Bellevue-Hopewell Highway).

17.0 Turn right into Maude Williamson State Park, an excellent lunch stop. Eventually return to the park entrance and turn left (north) on **Highway 221**.

18.0 Turn left on **Bellevue-Hopewell Highway** (sign points to Hopewell).

19.3 Hopewell. Stay on the main road as it bears right (northwest).

21.4 Turn left at a sign pointing to Amity, staying on the Bellevue-Hopewell Highway (unmarked). When the road enters Amity at mile 25.5, it becomes **Nursery Avenue**.

26.0 Amity (store). Turn right on **Trade Street** (Highway 99W). (For a short side trip to an Amity city park, turn left on Fourth Street at mile 26.2.)

27.2 Turn right on **Highway 233**. At mile 32.3, follow Highway 233 when it bears left at an intersection with Starr Quarry Road, and stay on Highway 233 through intersections at miles 33.8 and 34.0.

34.6 Ride straight (northeast) through an intersection with Lafayette Highway, leaving Highway 233, which turns left. You are now on a road known variously as **Highline Road** or **Amity-Dayton Highway**. When it reaches Dayton, it becomes **Ferry Street**.

36.3 Corner of Ferry and Third streets in Dayton. End of ride.

Yamhill County

22 EOLA HILLS

Starting Point: Maude William-
son State Park, midway between
Salem and Dayton on State
Highway 221.
Distance: 34.7 miles.
Terrain: Moderate with one
severe hill.
**Total Cumulative Elevation
Gain:** 1200 feet.
Recommended Time of Year:
Any season.
Recommended Starting Time:
Before noon.
Allow: 3 to 4 hours.

Points of Interest
Maude Williamson State Park
Willamette Greenway parks
Eola Hills
Hidden Springs Winery

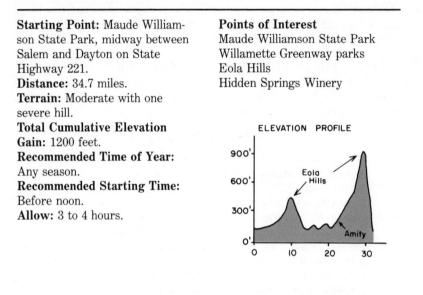

ELEVATION PROFILE

The Willamette Valley is noted for flat farm roads, but tucked away in a few corners of the valley are long, steep hills for energetic riders. Oddly enough, some of these climbs are found not in the foothills of the Cascades or the Coast Range but in the heart of the valley only a few miles from the river. Two examples are the Chehalem Mountains near Newberg (Trip #19) and the Eola Hills west of Salem.

The Eola Hills form a 13-mile ridge from Salem north almost to Mc-Minnville. The thousand-foot crest of the ridge is breached by two 450-foot passes—one at Spring Valley between the communities of Lincoln and Bethel, and the other between Grand Island and Amity.

The route described here starts near Grand Island, follows the Willamette upstream to Lincoln, then crosses the pass at Spring Valley. Once on the west side of the ridge, the route moves north through rolling farmland to Amity.

At Amity, the rider has the choice of crossing the second 450-foot pass or climbing to a crest twice as high. The choice is easy, right? Wrong. Waiting at the top of that thousand-foot ridge are some of the finest views around. The entire Willamette Valley will be spread out before you, with Grand Island at your feet and the Cascades shimmering in the distance. Not enough, huh? How about an exhilarating descent on a narrow farm road? Still not enough? How about wine tasting at a vineyard near the summit? What more could you ask for? Whatever your preference, routes over both the thousand-foot ridge and the 450-foot pass are described below.

Presuming the climbs over the Eola Hills don't wear you out, you may take several side trips. Amity Vineyards offer wine tasting at its winery just north of the route, and you won't have to climb a thousand-foot ridge to get there. From Amity, turn north 0.4 mile on Trade Street (Highway 99W), then turn right on Rice Lane.

Another diversion is offered just a mile east of the route, where the Wheatland Ferry makes its crossing of the Willamette. The ferry boat, the *Daniel Matheny IV*, is named after the founder of Wheatland who originated the ferry service in 1844. Although motorists are charged a small toll, bicyclists and pedestrians ride for free.

MILEAGE LOG

0.0 Maude Williamson State Park. Ride toward the park entrance, then turn south on **Highway 221**.

2.4 Spring Valley Access (Willamette River Greenway) is on the left, at the end of a 0.4-mile road (day use only; no drinking water).

5.6 Lincoln Access (Willamette River Greenway) is on the left, at the end of 0.4-mile Lincoln Road (day use only; no drinking water).

5.7 Lincoln (store). Turn right on **Zena Road**. At mile 7.7, follow Zena Road when it curves northwest at an intersection with Brush College Road and Spring Valley Road. Cross Highway 99W at mile 13.1, where Zena Road becomes **Bethel Road**.

13.6 McCoy (store).

15.6 Perrydale. Continue west on **West Perrydale Road** (Byerley Corner Road).

16.0 Turn right (north) on **Broadmead Road**.

18.3 At a T-intersection with **Ballston Road**, turn right.

21.4 Ballston Road joins **Bellevue-Hopewell Highway**; continue straight (north) at a stop sign, following signs pointing to Amity.

23.7 Amity (store). Turn right (south) on **Highway 99W** (Trade Street).

23.8 Turn left on **Nursery Avenue**, which reacquires the name **Bellevue-Hopewell Highway** after leaving Amity.

24.6 Turn right (south) on **Bethel Road**. (For an alternate route, and a less severe hill, continue straight, climb over a 450-foot pass, then follow Bellevue-Hopewell Highway when it turns right at a T-intersection at mile 28.4.)

25.6 Turn left on an unmarked road (**Eola Hills Road**), which climbs 800 feet in the next 3.5 miles. The crest of the hill is reached at mile 29.1, and Hidden Springs Winery is on the right at mile 30.0. The road begins a steep descent at mile 30.8.

31.3 When Eola Hills Road bears left, bear right on **County Road 556**.

32.0 Turn right at a T-intersection with **Bellevue-Hopewell Highway**. At mile 33.0, the road curves left and passes through the town of

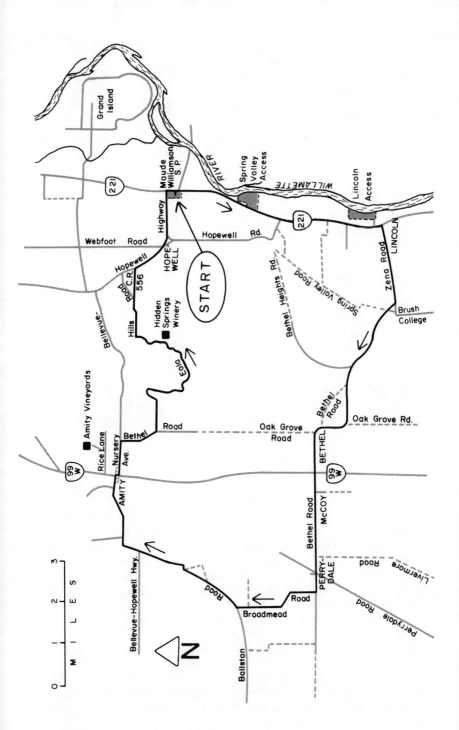

START

Grand Island

Maude Williamson S.P.

Spring Valley Access

Lincoln Access

WILLAMETTE

RIVER

221

221

Highway

Webfoot Road

Hopewell Rd.

Hopewell

Hopewell

HOPEWELL

C.R. 556

Rood

Bethel Heights Rd.

Spring Valley Road

Zena Road

LINCOLN

Brush College

Hidden Springs Winery

Bellevue-

Hills

Eola

Amity Vineyards

Rice Lane

Nursery Ave.

Bethel

Road

Oak Grove Road

Oak Grove Rd.

Bethel Road

BETHEL

99 W

99 W

AMITY

Bethel Road

McCOY

PERRY-DALE

Livermore Road

Bellevue-Hopewell Hwy.

Road

Road

Broadmead

Ballston

Perrydale Road

N

M I L E S

0   1   2   3

Hopewell, which consists almost entirely of an 1880 church and a turn-of-the-century schoolhouse.

34.4 Turn right (south) at a T-intersection with **Highway 221**.

34.6 Turn right into Maude Williamson State Park.

34.7 Maude Williamson State Park. End of ride.

Yamhill County

23 UPPER YAMHILL VALLEY

Starting Point: Grenfell Park, two miles west of Sheridan on State Highway 18. Turn south on Harmony Road, then turn west into the park.
Distance: 32.1 miles.
Terrain: Mixed hilly and flat.
Total Cumulative Elevation Gain: 1100 feet.
Recommended Time of Year: Any season.
Recommended Starting Time: Before noon.
Allow: 3 hours.

Points of Interest
Grenfell Park
Buell Park
Ballston Park

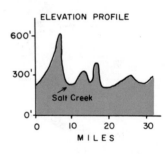

The South Yamhill River has its source in the Coast Range, barely 10 miles from the Pacific. It is a mountain stream for its first few miles, but after passing the town of Sheridan it meanders its way through a broad valley of flat farmland. The ride starts in the valley near Sheridan and circles through the foothills south of the river. Much of the ride is level, but the crossing of a 600-foot ridge between Mill Creek and Salt Creek will require some extra effort.

The ride starts in Yamhill County, just outside of Sheridan, then crosses into Polk County and stays there most of the distance. Three small parks are visited along the way. The starting point, Grenfell Park, is on Mill Creek, as is Buell Park, five miles later. The third park, in the tiny town of Ballston, boasts an equally tiny, yet well-preserved, 1865 schoolhouse.

The route passes several other historic buildings, including grange halls, schoolhouses, and churches, at least one of which is complete with a church-

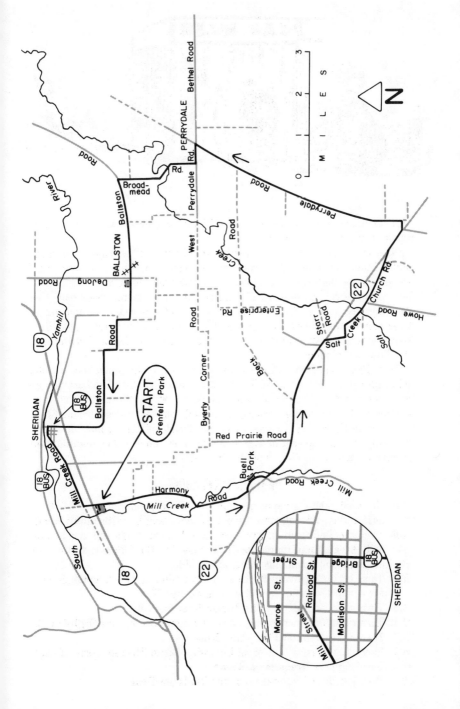

101

yard cemetery. You will also see some Victorian houses in various states of repair, particularly near Perrydale.

Several miles of the route follow State Highway 22, a major auto route and officially designated bike route to the coast from the Salem area. This section of the highway is also part of the Bikecentennial transcontinental bike route. Although auto traffic can be heavy on summer weekends, the shoulders are wide and the experience not at all unpleasant. At mile 9.2, a three-mile detour parallels Highway 22 on Salt Creek Church Road. Hurried riders can stay on Highway 22 if they prefer the fast and straight to the slow and winding.

From Perrydale, two other routes described in this guidebook can be followed to the east. Eola Hills (Trip #22) circles the farmland (and steep hills) northeast of Perrydale, while Rickreall (Trip #29) circles the area southeast of Perrydale. Another possible side trip visits Basket Slough National Wildlife Refuge, three miles southeast of this route on State Highway 22. But the best diversion of all is west, up over the mountains on Highways 22 and 18, then down to the coast.

MILEAGE LOG

0.0 Grenfell Park (camping permitted; drinking water available). Ride east to the park entrance, then turn right (south) on **Harmony Road**.

4.6 One block before an intersection with Highway 22 (store), turn left on **Mill Creek Road** (unmarked). At mile 5.0, Buell Park is on the left (day use only; drinking water available).

5.3 Turn left on **Highway 22**. The highway climbs a mile-long hill, is level for a short section, then descends a long hill.

9.2 Turn right on **Salt Creek Church Road** (store).

12.1 Turn right (east) when Salt Creek Church Road rejoins **Highway 22**.

12.7 Turn left (north) on **Perrydale Road**.

18.6 Perrydale. Turn left on **West Perrydale Road** (Byerley Corner Road).

19.1 Turn right on **Broadmead Road**.

21.3 Turn left at a T-intersection with **Ballston Road**.

23.8 Ballston (store). Continue westbound.

23.9 Ballston Park (day use only; no drinking water) is on the right.

24.7 Follow Ballston Road (Ball Road) through the first of several 90-degree turns. Eventually the road curves north toward Sheridan.

28.8 Ballston Road joins **Highway 18B**. Continue north on an overpass across Highway 18, where Ballston Road (Highway 18B) becomes **Bridge Street** in Sheridan.

29.4 Turn left on **Railroad Street**.

29.6 Turn left on **Mill Street**. After leaving Sheridan, Mill Street becomes **Mill Creek Road**.

30.5 At a Y-intersection, bear right on Mill Creek Road.

31.5 Follow Mill Creek Road when it turns left (south) at an intersection with two gravel roads. Mill Creek Road eventually becomes **Harmony Road**.

31.9 After crossing Highway 18, turn right into Grenfell Park.

32.1 Grenfell Park. End of ride.

Marion County

24 FRENCH PRAIRIE

Starting Point: Champoeg State Park, reached by driving west from I-5 exit 278 or 282. Park at the visitor center near the park entrance.

Distance: 48.7 miles.

Terrain: Flat.

Total Cumulative Elevation Gain: 500 feet.

Recommended Time of Year: Any season.

Recommended Starting Time: 10:00 A.M.

Allow: 5 hours.

Points of Interest
Champoeg State Park
Numerous historic houses
St. Paul Catholic Church
St. Louis Catholic Church
Aurora Colony Historic District

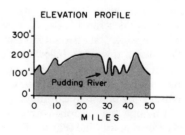

Although the Willamette River generally travels in a northerly direction, when it reaches Newberg it makes a pronounced turn to the east, travelling east for about a dozen miles to the Canby area. In so turning, the

Willamette cradles a broad plain of about 150 square miles known as French Prairie.

In many ways, French Prairie is one of the most historic areas of the Willamette Valley. The prairie was first inhabited by Calapooya Indians, who recognized its fine hunting, pasture, and fishing opportunities. When French-Canadians came to Oregon with the Hudson's Bay Company, many chose to settle French Prairie after retiring from the company. The first French-Canadians settled in 1829, and by 1845 the population numbered nearly seven hundred. Their agricultural successes resulted in the building of a grain warehouse on the river at an Indian camp called Champoeg. A sizable town grew up and was the site of a series of meetings in 1843 that resulted in the formation of a provisional government for the territory. The territory progressed toward statehood and prosperity, but the town was destroyed by the floods of 1861 and 1890.

The former townsite is now a huge (and hugely popular) state park, with extensive camping and picnic grounds, three small museums, and broad pastures complete with grazing sheep. This ride starts at the entrance to the park, near a recently constructed visitor center built in the style of a Willamette Valley barn.

French Prairie has retained much of its early character. The area is still mainly agricultural, and many of the farmhouses are well over a century old. The most imposing building in the area is the St. Paul Catholic Church, a towering brick structure built in 1846 to replace a log chapel.

On the east side of the prairie, the town of Aurora offers other historic buildings, many dating from the 1850s and 1860s when Aurora was operated as a communal colony under the strict leadership of Dr. William Keil.

This ride generally follows a route designated by the state's Parks and Recreation Branch as the French Prairie Loop. A brochure describing the route, and providing details on some of the historic buildings passed, is available from the Parks and Recreation Branch, Department of Transportation, Salem, Oregon, 97310. In addition to publishing the brochure, the state has marked the route with occasional fleur-de-lis directional signs. The route described below, however, differs from the official loop in one section: while the official loop travels Highway 99E between Gervais and Woodburn, this route follows backroads west of Highway 99E.

Unfortunately, the area has several inaccurate road signs and confusing road names, and the fleur-de-lis signs are few and far between. Use the mileage log and map carefully.

Although the described route is nearly 50 miles long, those seeking a shorter ride will find that the flat terrain of French Prairie and the general grid pattern of the roads lend themselves to a ride of almost any length. From nearly any point on the route, a relatively direct return to Champoeg can be made, particularly because few of the roads are heavily trafficked.

Even shorter rides are available on the bike paths of Champoeg State Park. In addition to the paths that stay within the main area of the park, a three-mile path runs east along the river to the small town of Butteville.

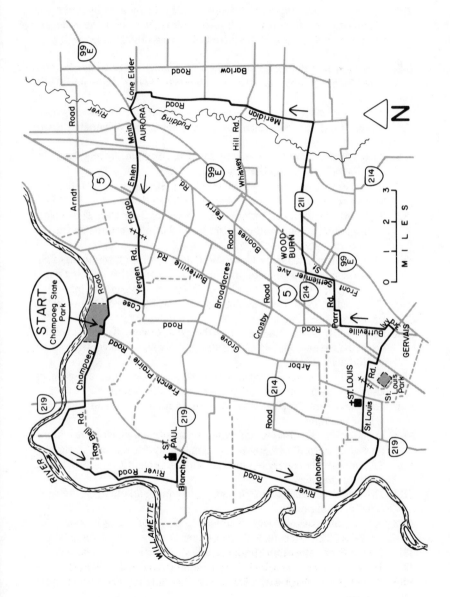

MILEAGE LOG

0.0 Champoeg State Park. Leave the park by turning right (west) on **Champoeg Road**. A bike path along the right side of the road extends 0.1 mile to the Robert Newell House (1852), now a D.A.R. museum.

0.2 Turn right at a T-intersection, following Champoeg Road north, then west. Ride straight (west) at an intersection with Highway 219 at mile 2.7.

2.8 Bear right at an intersection with Ray Bell Road. Follow this road (**River Road**) for several miles as it follows the Willamette River toward St. Paul.

9.7 Turn left at a T-intersection with **Blanchet Avenue**. At mile 10.7, St. Paul Catholic Church (1846) is on the left.

10.8 Turn right at an intersection with **Main Street** in St. Paul. After leaving St. Paul, Main Street becomes **River Road**.

18.7 Turn left (north) at a T-intersection with **Highway 219**. The Nusom House (1904) stands on the south side of this intersection. On the left at mile 19.1 stands an 1864 barn.

19.4 Turn right on **St. Louis Road** and follow it through the town of St. Louis at mile 20.4. Located a half-block north of this intersection is the St. Louis Catholic Church (ca. 1880). On the right at mile 21.1, Tesch Road leads to public fishing ponds at St. Louis County Park.

22.0 Cross I-5 on an overpass.

23.0 Gervais. St. Louis Road becomes **Douglas Avenue**. Turn left (north) on **Third Street**, leaving the official state loop, which continues east to Highway 99E.

23.3 Follow the arterial as it turns left (west) on **Ivy Avenue**. A few blocks later, Ivy turns north and becomes **Butteville Road**.

25.0 Just before an overpass with I-5, turn right on **Parr Road** and follow it into Woodburn.

26.8 Turn left on **Settlemier Avenue** (unmarked) one block before an intersection with Front Street. Settlemier City Park is on the right at 27.1 miles. The route rejoins the state's official loop a few blocks north of the park.

27.8 Turn right on **Highway 214**, using a bike path and lane on the right side of the highway.

29.2 At an intersection with Highway 99E, ride straight (east) on **Highway 211**. At mile 31.1, cross a bridge over the Pudding River.

33.0 Turn left on **Meridian Road** and follow it north for several miles.

39.5 Turn left at an unmarked T-intersection (**Lone Elder Road**).

40.0 Turn left on **Highway 99E**, cross the Pudding River, and enter Aurora.

40.4 Turn right on **Main Street** (unmarked). The road eventually becomes **Ehlen Road**, then **Fargo Road**, then changes to **Yergen Road** as it proceeds west through intersections with Boones Ferry Road, I-5, Butteville Road, and Donald Road.

46.8 Turn right (north) at an intersection with **Case Road**.

48.2 Turn left on **Champoeg Road**.

48.7 Turn right into Champoeg State Park. End of ride.

Marion County

25 SOUTH FRENCH PRAIRIE

Starting Point: Wheatland Park, in Marion County on the east side of the Willamette River at the Wheatland Ferry. From I-5 exit 263, drive west through Hopmere, turn north on Wheatland Road, then turn west on Matheny Road.
Distance: 32.8 miles.
Terrain: Flat.
Total Cumulative Elevation Gain: 575 feet.
Recommended Time of Year: Any season.
Recommended Starting Time: Before noon.
Allow: 3 to 4 hours.

Points of Interest
Wheatland Ferry
St. Louis Catholic Church
St. Louis fish ponds
Mount Angel
Willamette Mission State Park

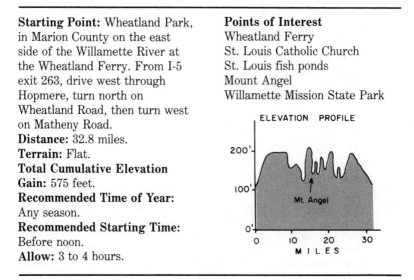

This 32-mile loop through farmland northeast of Salem offers fine riding, little traffic, and a variety of diversions along the way. For those who like to ride hard and fast, the route offers relatively flat roads with occasional small hills but without any traffic to worry about. For those who prefer to take their time, the route offers numerous parks, small towns, and old cemeteries as distractions.

The route visits several parks, two of which are quite large. But the ride begins and ends at Wheatland County Park, which is little more than a gravel parking lot along the river. Although Wheatland was once a sizable community, all that remains is the Wheatland Ferry; it has been operating since 1844.

Farther east on the ride, the large St. Louis County Park consists of seven man-made fishing ponds that have been stocked with catfish, bass, bluegill, and crappie. The large ponds seem completely out of place in the

Willamette Valley farmland, which has relatively few lakes and ponds.

The other large park is Willamette Mission State Park, with its sprawling wheat fields, filbert orchards, and the site of Jason Lee's 1834 Methodist mission. Today, the lowlands between Wheatland and Salem are still known as Mission Bottom.

Several interesting old cemeteries can be visited on this trip. The St. Louis cemetery, lying a few blocks north of the route, is one of the oldest in the state. Its residents include Madame Marie Dorion, the first pioneer woman to settle in the Oregon Territory. Just east of Gervais, two small cemeteries straddle the route. Both contain a variety of tombstones from this century and the last. On the south side of the road, the Masonic cemetery includes two sections of Russian graves, several of which are marked with the distinctive cross of the Russian Orthodox Christian Church.

Farther east, the route passes through the western edge of Mount Angel. Visible from more than a mile away, this town is part of a picturesque scene — a small farm community centered around a towering church steeple, with a beautiful wooded knoll in the background.

MILEAGE LOG

0.0 Wheatland Park. Ride east on **Matheny Road**.

0.4 At a T-intersection, turn left, staying on Matheny Road. Wheatland Road is on the right.

3.6 Turn left at a T-intersection with **Highway 219** (River Road).

5.8 Turn right on **St. Louis Road**. At mile 6.7, the St. Louis cemetery is visible off to the left. At mile 6.9, pass through the town of St. Louis at an intersection with Manning Road. One-half block north on Manning Road is the St. Louis Catholic Church (ca. 1880). At mile 7.4, St. Louis County Park is on the right. The road into the fish ponds is about a mile long, the first half of which is paved. At mile 8.4, cross I-5 on an overpass.

9.3 St. Louis Road enters Gervais and becomes **Douglas Street**. Continue straight through Gervais. After crossing Highway 99E at mile 9.9, the road becomes **Mt. Angel-Gervais Road**. At mile 10.3, small cemeteries lie on both sides of the road.

11.3 Turn right (south) at a T-intersection with **Howell Prairie Road**.

11.4 Turn left on **Mt. Angel-Gervais Road**. At mile 13.1, cross a bridge over the Pudding River.

14.5 Turn right at an intersection with Baron Road and Dominic Road. At mile 15.5, the road turns left toward Mount Angel and becomes **Marquam Street**. At mile 15.7, Ebner County Park is on the left at the end of a short side street.

15.9 Turn right on **Lincoln Street**.

16.1 Turn right on **Church Street**. Mount Angel city center is one block east of this intersection.

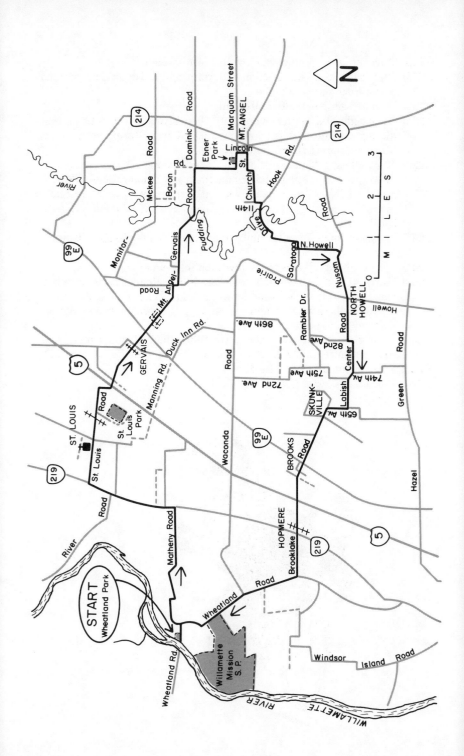

17.5 Turn left at a T-intersection with **114th Avenue**.

17.6 Turn right at an intersection with **Saratoga Drive** on the right and Hook Road on the left.

19.4 Turn left on **North Howell Road**.

20.5 Turn right at a T-intersection with **Nusom Road**. At mile 21.7, pass through an intersection known as North Howell (store) where Nusom Road becomes **Labish Center Road**.

22.7 Turn left at a T-intersection with **82nd Avenue**. A block later, the road turns west again and regains the name **Labish Center Road**.

23.5 Follow Labish Center Road when it turns right at an intersection with 74th Avenue. Cross a bridge over the Little Pudding River a block later.

23.7 Labish Center. Bear left, following Labish Center Road as it heads west.

24.5 Turn right at a T-intersection with **65th Avenue**.

25.0 Turn left at a T-intersection with **Brooklake Road**. This intersection has the distinction of being known as Skunkville. Follow Brooklake Road for the next several miles, through the town of Brooks at mile 26.4 and Hopmere at mile 28.1.

29.2 Turn right at a T-intersection with **Wheatland Road**. At mile 31.6, the entrance to Willamette Mission State Park is on the left.

32.4 Turn left on **Matheny Road**.

32.8 Wheatland Park. End of ride.

26 MOUNT ANGEL FOOTHILLS

Starting Point: St. Mary's Church, in Mount Angel on Church Street between Oak and Elm streets. Park along the south side of Church Street.
Distance: 38.5 miles.
Terrain: Mixed hilly and flat.
Total Cumulative Elevation Gain: 1750 feet.
Recommended Time of Year: Any season.
Recommended Starting Time: 10:00 A.M.
Allow: 4 to 5 hours.

Point of Interest
Mount Angel Abbey

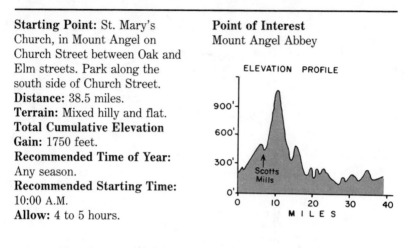

The foothills and farmland around Mount Angel provide fine bicycling over varied terrain. The farmland offers bicycling on typical Willamette Valley farm roads, and the foothills offer fine views of the valley. Roughly one-third of this ride is in the foothills, and the rest travels the flat farm roads. Both places are nearly devoid of traffic.

The farms passed are as varied as the terrain: look for hop fields and filbert orchards in the flatlands, Christmas tree farms in the hills, and berry and pumpkin patches in-between.

The population of the Mount Angel area is equally varied. Many of the residents are Catholic, descended from the French-Canadians who settled the area in the 1830s. Another segment of the population consists of Russian Old Believers, who fled religious persecution by travelling to Brazil and New Jersey and then to the Willamette Valley. Still another group is of Mexican descent, as evidenced by the many bilingual signs in Mount Angel.

A less authentic ethnic touch comes from the efforts the town is making to create the atmosphere of a Bavarian village, complete with ersatz chalet architecture, German signs, and an annual "Oktoberfest" in mid-September. The festival, by the way, attracts throngs of high-spirited celebrants; it is not a good time for bicyclists to visit the area. Otherwise, fall colors make this a fine autumn ride.

The starting point for the ride is not hard to find: just look for the huge steeple a few blocks east of the center of Mount Angel. The ride proceeds east from the steeple's church, over a shoulder of the knoll on which Mount Angel Abbey sits. A side trip to the top of the knoll offers fine views of the valley and a look at a Benedictine monastery that was established in 1884.

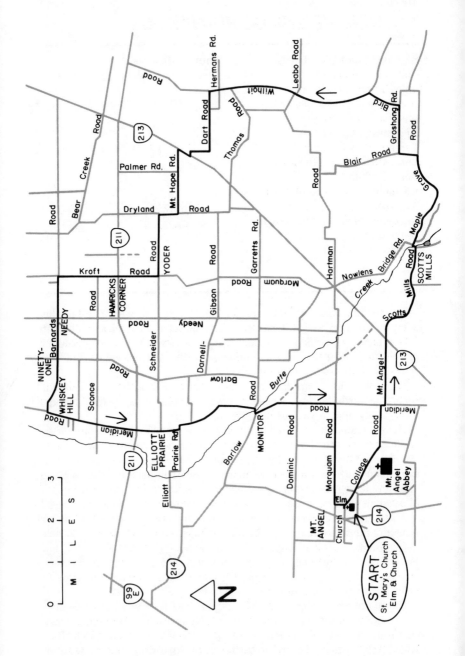

Many of the monastery's buildings are fine examples of neo-Romanesque architecture. The most notable exception, its library, was designed by the Finnish architect Alvar Aalto and completed in 1970. It alone is worth the trip. Another special feature is a small new museum devoted to the history of the Russian Old Believers.

After a few miles of flat farmland, the route climbs the end of a small ridge, then drops into a sleepy little hollow and the town of Scotts Mills. After crossing Butte Creek, the grade steepens considerably as the route climbs "Missouri Ridge," then drops into the Rock Creek Valley. Rock Creek is followed north several miles into farmland that steadily grows flatter and flatter. Nonexistent "towns" are visited, with curious names like Needy, Ninety One, and Whiskey Hill.

Since the roads through the farmland are basically in a grid pattern, several shortcuts are available for cyclists who do not want to pedal the full 38.5 miles. For example, from the Yoder area, a rider can easily pedal south and west to return to Mount Angel.

MILEAGE LOG

0.0 St. Mary's Church in Mount Angel. Ride east on **Church Street**, which soon becomes **College Street** and later **College Road**. At mile 0.6, the entrance to Mount Angel Abbey is on the right.

2.7 Turn right on **Meridian Road**, then a block later turn left on **Mount Angel-Scotts Mills Road**. Ride straight (east) through Lone Pine Corner at mile 4.3.

6.9 Scotts Mills (store). Mount Angel-Scotts Mills Road becomes **Third Street**. Scotts Mills Area Historical Society Museum (an old church) is located one block north on Grandview Avenue. Scotts Mills County Park is located a quarter mile south of town on Crooked Finger Road. Continue east on Third Street and cross Nowlens Bridge on the east edge of town, where Third Street becomes **Nowlens Bridge Road**.

7.1 Turn right on **Maple Grove Road** (Scotts Mills Road) and follow it as it climbs Missouri Ridge.

9.6 Turn left on **Blair Road**.

10.1 Bear right (east) on **Groshong Road**.

11.2 Turn left on **Bird Road**, which makes a rapid drop into the Rock Creek Valley. Beware of tight corners and wet leaves.

12.1 Turn left at a T-intersection with **Wilhoit Road** and follow it as it glides down the Rock Creek Valley.

16.3 Turn left on **Dart Road** and follow it through farmland west and north to Highway 213.

18.3 Turn right on **Highway 213**. Watch for moderate traffic.

18.6 Turn left on **Mount Hope Road**.

20.1 At a T-intersection with **Dryland Road**, turn right.

20.6 Turn left on **Schneider Road**.

22.1 Yoder. Turn right on **Kroft Road** and follow it north through

Hamricks Corner at mile 23.1. At mile 23.5, Smyrna Church (1891) stands on the left.

24.6 Turn left on **Barnards Road** and follow it west through the communities of Needy and Ninety One.

28.0 Whiskey Hill. Turn left on **Meridian Road**. At mile 30.9, pass through the community of Elliot Prairie. At mile 31.4, stay on Meridian Road when it jogs left at an intersection with Elliot Prairie Road.

33.5 At a T-intersection with **Barlow Road**, turn right, cross a bridge over Butte Creek, and enter the town of Monitor.

33.6 Turn left on **Meridian Road**. Continue through an intersection with Dominic Road at mile 34.7.

35.7 Turn right on **Marquam Road** and follow it into Mount Angel.

38.1 Turn left on **Elm Street**.

38.4 T-intersection. Church Street is on the right, College Street on the left. Turn right on **Church Street**.

38.5 St. Mary's Church. End of ride.

Marion County

27 SILVER CREEK

Starting Point: Coolidge & McClaine Park, at the corner of Charles Avenue and Coolidge Street in Silverton. From State Highway 214 in downtown Silverton, turn left on Main Street, then turn left on Coolidge Street.
Distance: 34.7 miles.
Terrain: Hilly.
Total Cumulative Elevation Gain: 2500 feet.
Recommended Time of Year: Any season, except during snowy conditions.
Recommended Starting Time: 10:00 A.M.
Allow: 4 to 5 hours.

Point of Interest
Silver Falls State Park

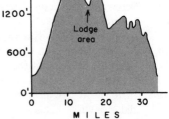

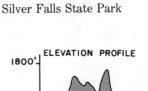

Silver Falls State Park is one of the largest and prettiest in the state park system. Noted for more than a dozen waterfalls, the park is justifiably popular, particularly in summer when the cool, mossy forests attract refugees from the heat of the Willamette Valley.

The park is open all year, and thus this ride can be made any season, but spring and fall are probably the best. In summer the park can often be crowded, and in winter many of the facilities are closed, including some of the park's footpaths and bike trails. During cold weather the roads may also be icy or covered with snow.

Opossums, which resemble large, gray rats, can frequently be seen along the roadside in wooded areas. The only marsupial native to North America, these unique mammals are not indigenous to the Northwest, but were introduced by settlers from the Ozarks who enjoyed hunting them. The adaptable little creatures have become a permanent part of Oregon fauna.

The ride starts in Coolidge & McClaine Park, a shady grove of trees just across Silver Creek from downtown Silverton. After crossing a pedestrian bridge, the route proceeds south along Silver Creek for about two miles,

*"No, I've never had any problems
with the 'possums...!"*

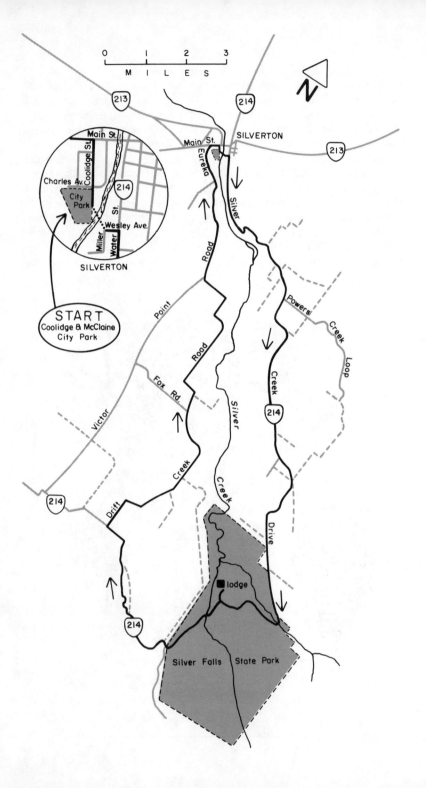

then begins to climb steeply up the side of the wooded valley, offering views of Silver Creek Reservoir. The winding road has no shoulders, so ride carefully.

After a mile or two of climbing, the road begins to level out, then traverses southeast along a ridge known as the Silverton Hills. Gently rolling tree farms and fine views to the south and west characterize this part of the ride. The highway gains several hundred feet of elevation as it climbs the ridge, but the gently undulating hills disguise the elevation gain.

Near mile 13, the route enters the heavily wooded state park, leaving behind the openness of the sprawling tree farms. The park offers a variety of activities, the two most popular being picnicking and hiking. Most of the picnic sites are in the central area of the park near the lodge; a swimming hole is nearby. The trails to the waterfalls are generally short and well graded, although a few involve some stairs. Either walk your bike along the trails or carry a lock and leave your bike at the trailhead. The highest falls in the park, South Falls (177 feet), are less than a half-mile walk from the lodge area.

From the park the route continues to climb to 1750 feet, then sweeps down through the woods to farmland at the head of Drift Creek. The final leg of the journey is perhaps the most scenic: the road runs north on a ridge between Drift Creek on the west and Silver Creek on the east, with dramatic views into the steeply sided Silver Creek Valley. Silver Creek disappears around a bend to the south, giving no hint of the dozen waterfalls hidden at the head of its valley.

MILEAGE LOG

0.0 Coolidge & McClaine Park in Silverton. Proceed south on **Coolidge Street** through the park.

0.1 Turn left and cross a footbridge over Silver Creek. At the far end of the bridge, bear right (southeast) and cross a parking lot.

0.2 Turn left (east) on **Wesley Avenue**.

0.3 At a T-intersection with **Water Street** (Highway 214), turn right (south). Follow this road for several miles. After leaving Silverton, Water Street becomes **Silver Creek Drive** but retains the Highway 214 designation.

12.9 Highway 214 enters Silver Falls State Park. A road on the right leads to a group campground. Continue southeast on Highway 214.

13.0 Bridge over the North Fork of Silver Creek. From the parking lot at this bridge, trails lead to North Falls and Upper North Falls. At mile 13.6, a short walk to the right gives a good view of North Falls. At mile 14.8, the road crosses a bike path. For an alternate route to the lodge and picnic area, turn right on the bike path.

15.7 Turn right into the central area of the park, where the lodge and picnic area are located. After lunch or exploration, return to this intersection and turn right (south).

22.4 Turn right (north) on **Drift Creek Road.** At mile 30.4, Drift Creek Road joins **Victor Point Road**, which eventually becomes **Eureka Street** after entering Silverton.

34.3 Turn right at a T-intersection with **Main Street.**

34.6 At the bottom of a hill, turn right on **Coolidge Street.**

34.7 Coolidge & McClaine Park. End of ride.

Marion County

28 NORTH SANTIAM

Starting Point: Jefferson Middle School, one mile north of Jefferson at the intersection of Talbot Road and Jefferson Highway. From I-5, use exit 242 or 244.

Distance: East loop — 33.9 miles. West loop — 34.5 miles.

Terrain: East loop — gentle. West loop — mixed hilly and flat.

Total Cumulative Elevation Gain: East loop — 775 feet. West loop — 1500 feet.

Recommended Time of Year: Any season.

Recommended Starting Time: Before noon for either loop; 10:00 A.M. for a combined loop.

Allow: 3 to 4 hours for either loop; 5 hours for a combined loop.

Points of Interest

Mill Creek
Turner Tabernacle
Ankeny National Wildlife Refuge
Buena Vista Ferry

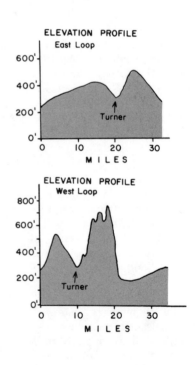

Southwestern Marion County is a mixture of flat farm country and steep hills. The hills, which run from Jefferson north toward Salem, divide the farmland. The eastern section borders on the twisting North Santiam River, while the western section, known as Ankeny Bottom, is surrounded by the Willamette and Santiam rivers.

When steamboats were plying the Willamette River prior to the turn of the century, Ankeny Bottom was an important source of fuel, because boats could pull in at landings, such as Sidney, to load a fresh supply of cordwood. Today, Sidney is just a cluster of houses nearly a mile from the river, and Ankeny Bottom is noted, not for its woodlots, but for a National Wildlife Refuge that occupies much of the Bottom.

Two routes, one flat and one hilly, are described here. The gentle east loop follows the North Santiam River upstream through corn and mint fields toward Stayton, then turns around and follows Mill Creek downstream. Along the way, it crosses Mill Creek at least eight times before turning south for the ride back to Jefferson. It also passes through several small towns, including Marion, Aumsville, and Turner.

According to *Oregon Geographic Names*, Marion and Turner have a common history. When a railroad worker was instructed to build a station and warehouse at a site on Mill Creek to be called Marion, the materials were mistakenly delivered to another site six miles farther down the line. The railroad realized the mistake but went ahead and used the new site and the name Marion, later building a station at the original site and giving it the name of Turner. Turner is now a sizable community, despite its early difficulties, while Marion, like Sidney, is just a sleepy little cluster of houses. Turner is also the location of a huge church, the Turner Tabernacle, on the east edge of town.

The hilly west loop also visits Turner, then rides west across the Salem Hills before turning south to Ankeny Bottom and the Buena Vista Ferry landing. A level route is then followed along the Santiam River back to Jefferson. Along the way, watch for a long row of black walnut trees and, in season, a road covered with walnuts.

MILEAGE LOG

EAST LOOP

0.0 Jefferson Middle School one mile north of Jefferson. Ride south on **Jefferson Highway**. A bike lane is available on the west side of the road.

0.5 Turn left, following the sign pointing to Marion and Stayton. This street (**North Avenue**) turns north at mile 0.7 and becomes **Marion Road**.

5.6 Marion (store). Turn right on **Stayton Road**.

11.1 Stayton Road merges with **West Stayton Road** (store). Continue eastbound.

13.1 Turn left (north) on **Wilco Road** (store). At mile 14.0, Wilco Road crosses Shaff Road and becomes **Golf Club Road**.

15.5 Immediately before an intersection with Highway 22, turn left on **Mill Creek Road**.

18.1 Mill Creek Road is named **Main Street** as it passes through Aumsville. At mile 18.4, a pretty city park is on the north side of the

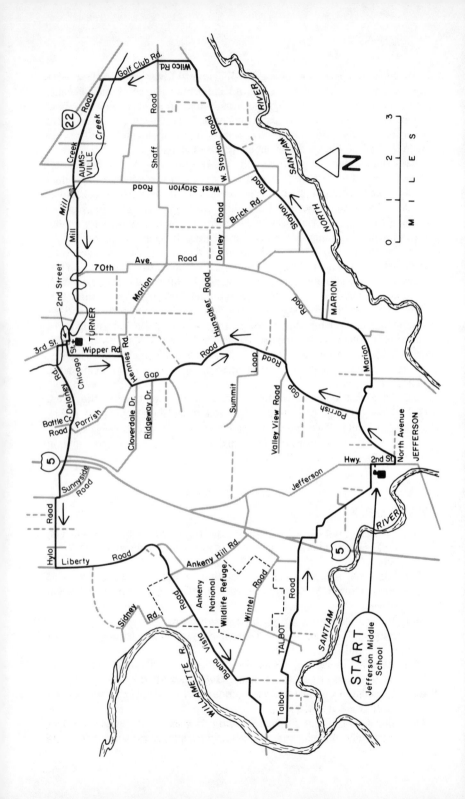

road in a grove of alders along Mill Creek (drinking water available). At mile 21.5, Mill Creek Road becomes **Marion Road**. The route passes the Turner Tabernacle at mile 22.0 and then becomes **Denver Street** in Turner.

22.2 Follow the arterial as it turns right on **Second Street**.

22.3 Follow the arterial as it turns left on **Chicago Street** one block later (store), then follow Chicago Street west out of town (store). At mile 22.6, Chicago Street turns south, crosses a small bridge, and becomes **Wipper Road**.

24.0 Turn right on **Hennies Road**.

24.7 Turn left (south) on **Parrish Gap Road** and follow it south for 7.0 miles.

31.7 Turn right at a T-intersection with **Marion Road**.

33.2 Marion Road curves right (west) and becomes **North Avenue** in Jefferson.

33.4 Turn right (north) on **Jefferson Highway** (Second Street).

33.9 Jefferson Middle School. End of ride.

WEST LOOP

0.0 Jefferson Middle School one mile north of Jefferson. Ride south on **Jefferson Highway**. A bike lane is available on the west side of the road.

0.5 Turn left, following the sign pointing to Marion and Stayton. This street (**North Avenue**) turns north at mile 0.7 and becomes **Marion Road**.

2.2 Turn left (north) on **Parrish Gap Road** and follow it north for 7.0 miles.

9.2 Turn right on **Hennies Road**.

9.9 Turn left (north) on **Wipper Road**. At mile 11.3, Wipper road turns east, enters Turner, and becomes **Chicago Street**.

11.6 Turner (store). Turn left (north) on **Third Street**.

11.8 Turn left on **Delaney Road**. At mile 13.9, follow Delaney Road when it turns left across a bridge at an intersection with Battle Creek Road. At mile 14.8, pass under I-5.

15.7 Turn right (north) at an intersection with **Sunnyside Road**.

15.8 Turn left on **Hylo Road**.

17.6 Turn left (south) on **Liberty Road**. At mile 21.3, the road enters Ankeny National Wildlife Refuge and becomes **Buena Vista Road**.

26.2 Turn left on **Talbot Road**. The Buena Vista Ferry landing is 0.3 mile west of this intersection.

31.3 Cross I-5 on an overpass, then bear right, following Talbot Road.

34.4 Turn right (south) at a T-intersection with **Jefferson Highway**.

34.5 Jefferson Middle School. End of ride.

29 RICKREALL

Starting Point: Holman
Wayside, four miles west of
Salem on State Highway 22.
Distance: 44.3 miles.
Terrain: Mixed hilly and flat.
**Total Cumulative Elevation
Gain:** 2200 feet.
Recommended Time of Year:
Any season.
Recommended Starting Time:
Before 10:00 A.M.
Allow: 5 hours.
Points of Interest
Eola Park
Brush College Park
Spring Valley
Historic churches
Dallas City Park
Polk County Courthouse
Polk Marine Park

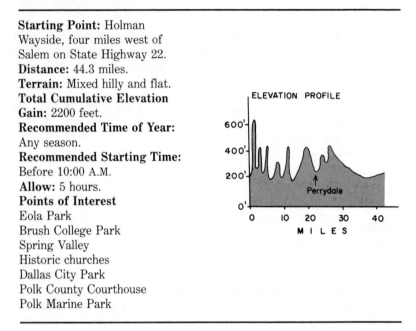

Rickreall Creek is a small stream that flows through the towns of Dallas and Rickreall before it enters the Willamette near Salem. Although the Dallas-Rickreall area is flat farmland, the area north of the Rickreall Valley is quite hilly. This route starts out by climbing those hills, then settles into the valley for the return leg.

The route comes within a short distance of two county parks and two city parks. The distance between the parks and the route ranges from a few feet to a half mile: take your pick of the ones you'd like to visit, but none of the side trips to the parks is included in the mileage of the loop described below.

The first park, Eola Park, is a large wooded tract near the start of the route. A narrow blacktop lane leads through the park in a one-mile horseshoe. A picnic area is located three-fourths of the way around the loop.

Brush College Park, a Salem city park, is near mile 3.9 of the route. This park was named for a local school, which in turn was named for the vegetation that still dominates the area.

Dallas City Park, the prettiest park on the ride, straddles Rickreall Creek just west of downtown Dallas. In Independence, Polk Marine Park gives access to the Willamette River. The park is on the east side of Independence, along State Highway 51.

The route passes several interesting old buildings. Three churches of

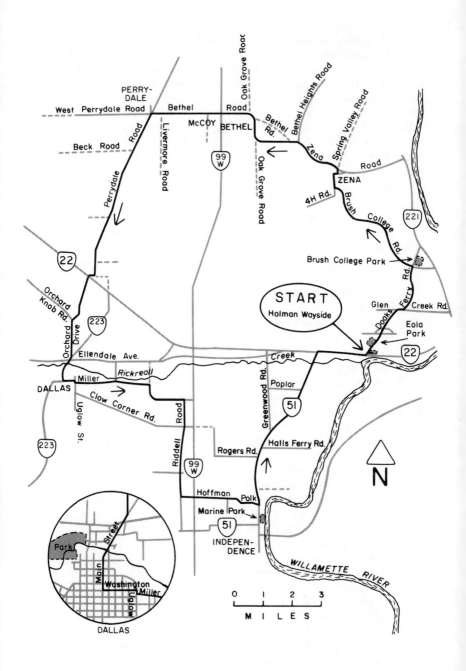

START
Holman Wayside

N

0   1   2   3
M I L E S

123

note can be seen at Zena, Bethel, and Perrydale. The Bethel church's architecture appears to be unusual for a church; older maps show that it was once a schoolhouse. Both Bethel and Zena are located in Spring Valley, surrounded by the Eola Hills. While the area seems isolated today, Spring Valley was once bustling when Doaks Ferry (now Lincoln) was the largest grain port on the upper Willamette.

Dallas also displays some interesting architecture. The route passes through the shadow of the Polk County Courthouse, or rather through the shadow of its ivy-covered clocktower, built in 1900 of limestone from a nearby quarry.

MILEAGE LOG

0.0 Holman Wayside (day use only; drinking water available). Leave the wayside and turn right (north) on **Doaks Ferry Road**. At mile 0.5, Eola Park (day use only; drinking water available) is on the left; a mile-long blacktop road leads through the park, then returns to Doaks Ferry Road.

2.1 Turn right on **Glen Creek Road** at a T-intersection.

2.4 At a fork in the road, bear left on **Doaks Ferry Road**.

3.9 Turn left on **Brush College Road**. Brush College Park (day use only; drinking water available) is immediately northeast of this intersection.

8.1 Follow Brush College Road when it turns right at an intersection with 4-H Road.

8.7 Turn left on **Spring Valley Road**, then turn left on **Zena Road**. At mile 14.0, cross Highway 99W; Zena Road becomes **Bethel Road**.

14.5 McCoy (store).

16.4 Perrydale. Turn left (south) on **Perrydale Road**. Cross Highway 22 at mile 22.3. Perrydale Road eventually becomes **Orchard Drive** in Dallas.

25.2 After entering Dallas, turn right at a T-intersection with **Highway 223** (Kings Valley Highway).

25.3 Carefully cross Ellendale Avenue at a major five-way intersection by bearing slightly to the right, following Highway 223 (Main Street) south. To visit Dallas City Park (day use only; drinking water available), turn right either on Walnut Avenue at mile 25.5 or on Academy Avenue at mile 25.7.

26.1 Turn left on **Washington Street**.

26.5 Turn right at a T-intersection with **Uglow Street**, then immediately turn left on **Miller Avenue**.

30.7 Turn right (south) on **Riddell Road**.

34.0 Turn left on **Hoffman Road**, then cross Highway 99W at mile 34.4. Hoffman Road becomes **Polk Street** when it enters Independence.

36.8 Turn left (north) on **Main Street** (Highway 51). (To visit Polk Marine Park in Independence, ride south 0.5 mile on Main Street, then turn left on B Street.)

42.7 Turn right (east) on **Highway 22**, using either the shoulder on the south side of the highway or the bike path on the north side.

44.2 Turn left on **Doaks Ferry Road**.

44.3 Turn right into Holman Wayside. End of ride.

Polk County

30 LUCKIAMUTE LOOPS

Starting Point: Monmouth City Park, at the corner of Main Street (State Highway 51) and Warren Street in Monmouth.

Distance: West loop — 28.7 miles. East loop — 28.5 miles.

Terrain: West loop — moderate. East loop — flat.

Total Cumulative Elevation Gain: West loop — 950 feet. East loop — 550 feet.

Recommended Time of Year: Any season.

Recommended Starting Time: Before noon for either one of the loops; 10:00 A.M. for a combined loop.

Allow: 3 hours for one loop; 5 hours for a combined loop.

Points of Interest
Sarah Helmick State Park
Buena Vista Park and Ferry
Polk Marine Park

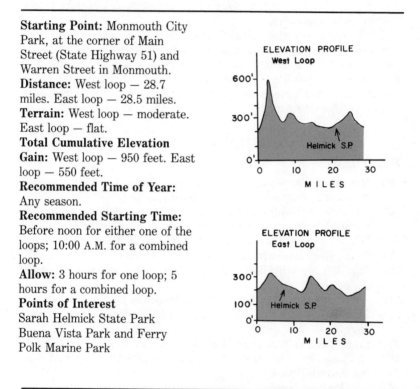

The Luckiamute River and its northern fork, the Little Luckiamute River, drain the southern half of Polk County, flowing from the Coast Range down to the flat farmland near Buena Vista and American Bottom. In the hills of the Coast Range, the two streams are clear and fast, but by the time they join and then cross the farmland south of Monmouth, the waters are muddy and the riverbed meandering.

Described below are two 28-mile loops that explore the lower Luckiamute Valley. The western loop skirts the edge of the Coast Range, but the few hills encountered are gentle. The eastern loop is relatively flat.

Both loops start in Monmouth, and both use a seven-mile road (Helmick Road) that runs south from Monmouth to Suver Junction. Either loop can be ridden by itself. Both loops can be ridden in a 57.2-mile day, or Helmick Road can be omitted and the perimeter of the two loops combined for a pleasant 41.8-mile ride.

Helmick Road, however, is one of the better parts of the two loops. Apparently an old section of Pacific Highway, it closely parallels State Highway 99W. The transcontinental Bikecentennial route follows Highway 99W through this area, but Helmick Road has much less traffic. In places its width was obviously designed for Model As, but the lack of traffic makes the narrowness immaterial.

Helmick Road also visits Sarah Helmick State Park, one of three riverfront parks visited by the two loops. One other is Buena Vista Park, a day use area on the Willamette just south of the Buena Vista ferry landing. The farmland just across the Willamette from Buena Vista is fine for biking, but the ferry doesn't run on weekends. The third park is Polk Marine Park, a block north of the main light in Independence on the east loop.

MILEAGE LOG

WEST LOOP

0.0 Monmouth City Park, at the corner of Warren and Main streets in Monmouth. Ride west on **Main Street** (Highway 51).

0.3 Turn left on **Whitman Street**, following the arterial (Monmouth Highway). About two miles later, the road climbs up over Fishback Hill, then drops down to the Little Luckiamute River.

7.4 Turn left on **Highway 223**.

8.5 Turn left on **Airlie Road**. At mile 14.9, pass through the town of Airlie (store).

21.0 Suver Junction. Turn left (north) on **Highway 99W**.

21.1 Bear left on an unmarked road (**Helmick Road**) that parallels Highway 99W.

23.8 Sarah Helmick State Park (day use only; drinking water available).

28.5 In Monmouth, bear left at a Y-intersection with Knox Street, following **Warren Street**.

28.7 City Park at corner of Warren and Main streets. End of ride.

EAST LOOP

0.0 Monmouth City Park at corner of Warren and Main streets. Ride south on **Warren Street**. After leaving Monmouth, Warren Street becomes **Helmick Road**.

4.9 Sarah Helmick State Park (day use only; drinking water available).

7.6 Continue south when Helmick Road joins **Highway 99W**.

7.7 Suver Junction. Turn left on **Suver Road**. At mile 8.5, the road passes through the tiny town of Suver.

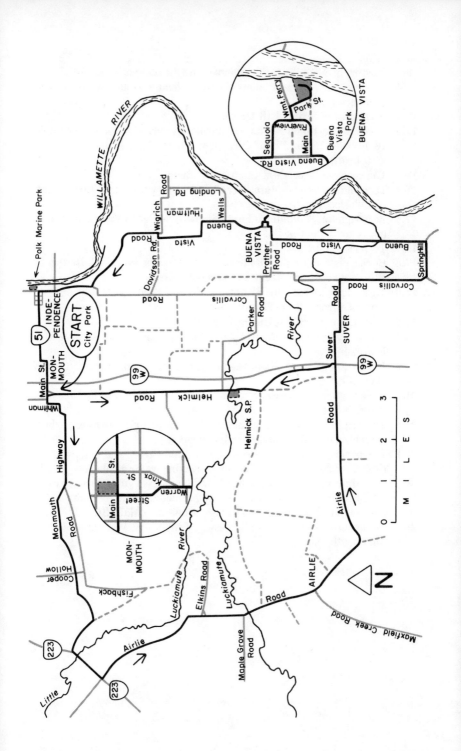

127

9.9 Turn right (south) at a T-intersection with **Corvallis Road**. (For a shortcut, turn left and follow Corvallis Road 8.6 miles north to Independence.)

12.1 Turn left on **Spring Hill Drive**.

13.0 Turn left (north) on **Buena Vista Road** (Buena Vista Street). At mile 16.9, follow Buena Vista Road when it turns right at an intersection with Prather Road.

17.3 The road turns north at the town of Buena Vista.

17.4 Turn right (east) on **Main Street**, then follow it when it turns north two blocks later.

17.6 Turn right on **Willamette Ferry Street**. The Buena Vista Ferry landing is at the foot of this street.

17.7 Turn right on **Park Street**.

17.8 Buena Vista Park (day use only; drinking water available). Return to **Willamette Ferry Street** and turn left (west).

18.0 Turn right (north) on **Riverview Street**, then follow the arterial when it turns left on **Sequoia Street**.

18.2 Turn right (north) on **Buena Vista Road**.

20.1 Follow Buena Vista Road when it turns left at an intersection with Hultman Road.

21.5 Follow Buena Vista Road when it turns right at an intersection with Davidson Road.

21.7 Follow Buena Vista Road when it turns left at an intersection with Wigrich Road.

24.3 Turn right (north) at a T-intersection with **Corvallis Road**, which soon becomes **Main Street** in Independence.

25.8 Independence, at the intersection of Main Street and Highway 51. (Polk Marine Park — day use only; drinking water available — can be visited by riding one block north on Main Street, then turning right on C Street.) The route turns left on **Monmouth Street** (Highway 51) and follows it to Monmouth, where it becomes **Main Street**.

28.5 Monmouth City Park at the corner of Main and Warren streets in Monmouth. End of ride.

31 LINN COUNTY COVERED BRIDGES

Starting Point: Jefferson Middle School, located one mile north of Jefferson at the intersection of Jefferson Highway and Talbot Road. From I-5, use exit 242 or 244.
Distance: 61.4 miles.
Terrain: Flat with two optional hills.
Total Cumulative Elevation Gain: 1400 feet.
Recommended Time of Year: Any season.
Recommended Starting Time: 9:00 A.M.
Allow: 6 hours.

Points of Interest
Eight covered bridges
Larwood County Wayside

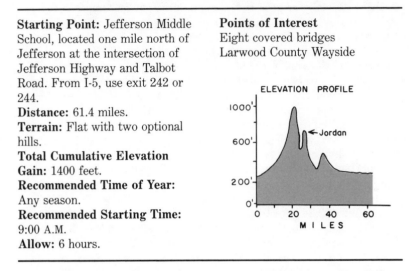

Long before the days of reinforced concrete and steel I-beams, Oregon's bridges were made of wood. Those days were also long before chemical preservatives came into use, and the bridges didn't last very long in the rainy weather of the Willamette Valley. This problem was solved by building roofs over the bridges and installing siding on their trusses. More than three hundred covered bridges once stood in Oregon, but eventually most were demolished in the face of increased traffic volume, heavier loads, and modern technology. Today, less than sixty survive.

In northwestern Linn County, not far from Albany, eight covered bridges stand within a few miles of each other. Of the eight, five cross Thomas Creek and three cross Crabtree Creek. Described below is a gerrymandered sixty-mile loop that crosses all eight bridges. Actually, the loop consists of three smaller loops with two or three bridges on each loop. For riders who do not wish to ride the full sixty miles, one or two of the loops may be omitted. The western loop, for example, permits riders to cross three bridges on a leisurely 35.1-mile route. The southeastern loop is a flat 10.6 miles that cross two bridges and visit a picturesque park at the community of Larwood. The northeastern loop climbs two steep hills but includes three bridges and some fine scenery along its 15.7 miles. For riders who may prefer to avoid the two hills, the mileage log describes two level alternate routes that shorten the loop by about three miles but still visit all of the bridges.

Like most covered bridges built in Oregon, the eight bridges crossed on this ride were built using Howe trusses, designed to incorporate diagonal timbers and vertical steel rods whose tension can be adjusted. Unlike most other counties, however, Linn County adopted a design that incorporates large windows or merely leaves the trusses exposed, shedding light where darkness normally reigns. For more information on Oregon's covered bridges, get a copy of *Roofs over Rivers* (Touchstone Press, 1978), a well-researched guide to the remaining bridges.

A bicycle is the best vehicle to use when touring the covered bridges, since many of them are closed to motor vehicles. The bridges protect riders from two seasonal enemies, cold rain and (somewhat less frequently) hot sun. Don't linger in the bridges too long, however, because all are narrow and offer little protection from oncoming traffic. The bridges were designed for Model As, not modern logging trucks. Even so, don't be surprised if you see a few dozen horseless carriages. Linn County's covered bridges are popular destinations for group outings of local antique car clubs.

Surprisingly, only one of the bridges on this ride is closed to motor vehicles, but all should be considered threatened by progress. As this book was going to press, the Jordan Bridge (mile 23.2) and the Bohemian Hall Bridge (mile 33.6) were being considered for demolition. In the last 20 years, perhaps two dozen of Oregon's covered bridges have been destroyed, while only four new ones have been built, and two of the four new ones were non-truss bridges that were covered with purely ornamental roofs. One of the other two, Shimanek Bridge, was built in 1966 and is crossed at mile 15.1 of this ride.

One other bridge near this route deserves mention. Just a block west of the route at the south end of Jefferson (mile 1.1) stands an example of engineering raised to an art form, a grand bridge erected in 1933 and dedicated to Jacob Conser, who founded Jefferson in 1851 and operated a ferry there for many years. The bridge, which consists of three 200-foot reinforced concrete through-arch spans, was designed by Conde B. McCullough. During his tenure as state bridge engineer from 1919 to 1938, McCullough supervised the design and construction of hundreds of bridges, large and small, but he is remembered best for his magnificent arch bridges on the Oregon coast.

P.S. This is a long ride, and drinking water is infrequently available. Be sure to carry enough.

MILEAGE LOG

0.0 Jefferson Middle School. Turn right (south) on **Jefferson Highway**, formerly Highway 99E, and follow it into the town of Jefferson, where it becomes **Second Street**.

1.1 Just after Second Street curves to the right (west), turn left on **Main Street**, which eventually becomes **Jefferson-Scio Drive**.

6.1 Turn right on **Robinson Drive**.

7.1 Turn right on **Goar Road** (Gore Road).

8.2 Gilkey Bridge.

*"Great! We can stop inside
and rest in the shade."*

8.5 Turn left (east) on **Gilkey Road** and follow it through several 90-degree turns.

11.8 Turn left at a T-intersection with **Highway 226** (unmarked) and follow it into Scio, where it becomes **Main Street**.

12.3 Scio (store). Turn right on **First Avenue**, following Highway 226.

14.4 Turn left (north) on **Richardsons Gap Road**.

15.1 Shimanek Bridge.

15.2 Continue straight past an intersection with County Road 639 (Shimanek Bridge Drive). (For those who want to shorten the ride and avoid an upcoming hill, turn right and follow C.R. 639 east 2.2 miles to Highway 226, then follow Highway 226 east past Hanna Bridge to Jordan Bridge, which appears below at mile 23.2.)

16.2 At the top of a long steep hill, turn right (east) on **Ridge Drive** (County Road 609).

16.3 Continue east on Ridge Drive at an intersection with Cole School Road.

19.9 Turn right on **Spring Valley Road**.

20.4 Turn right at a T-intersection with **Valley View Road**. At mile 20.7, the road curves left (east) and begins to descend into the Thomas Creek valley.

22.2 Turn right at a T-intersection with **Kingston-Jordan Drive**.

22.6 Bear right on **Highway 226**.

23.2 Turn left (south) on **Jordan Road**, cross Jordan Bridge, then climb a steep hill. (For those riders who wish to avoid the hill, continue west

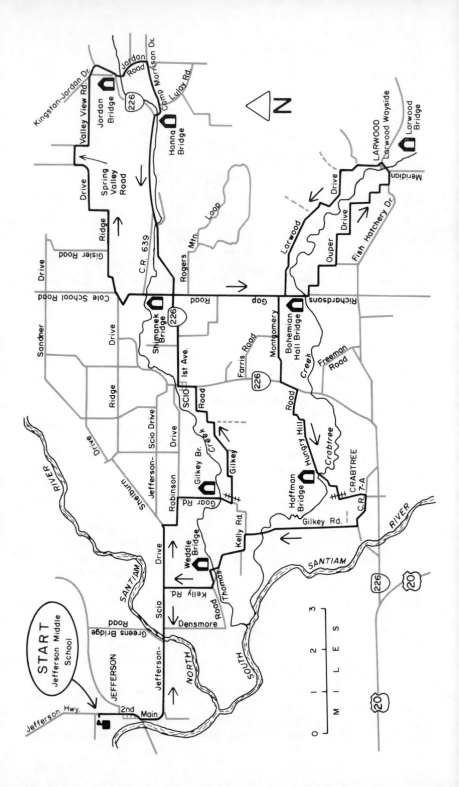

1.7 miles on Highway 226 to Hanna Bridge, described below at mile 25.7.)

24.2 Jordan. Turn right at a T-intersection with **Camp Morrison Drive**.

25.7 Hanna Bridge.

25.8 Turn left (west) at a T-intersection with **Highway 226**.

30.1 Turn left (south) at an intersection with **Richardsons Gap Road**.

33.6 Bohemian Hall Bridge.

33.7 Turn left on **Ouper Drive** (County Road 644) and follow it east and south through several 90-degree turns.

38.1 Turn left at a T-intersection with **Fish Hatchery Drive**. Bear left at an intersection with Meridian Road at mile 38.2.

38.4 Larwood Bridge.

38.5 Larwood. Turn left on **Larwood Drive** (County Road 643). Larwood County Wayside (no drinking water) is on the left, at the junction of Crabtree Creek and the Roaring River. Follow Larwood Drive as it winds north and west for several miles.

43.3 Turn right (north) at a T-intersection with **Richardsons Gap Road**.

43.5 Turn left on **Montgomery Drive**.

45.5 Turn left (south) on **Highway 226**.

46.0 Turn right on **Hungry Hill Road**.

48.3 Hoffman Bridge.

49.8 Crabtree. Turn right (west) at a T-intersection with **County Road 7-A** (Crabtree Drive, unmarked).

50.7 Turn right (north) on an unmarked road (**Gilkey Road**, County Road 7-A).

53.5 At a T-intersection, turn left on **Kelly Road**.

54.9 Shortly before crossing a modern highway bridge, turn right on an unmarked road and cross an automobile barrier.

55.1 Weddle Bridge.

55.2 Follow the old road as it turns left, then turn right at an intersection with the new road (**Kelly Road**). At mile 55.5, follow Kelly Road (County Road 622) as it turns right (north).

56.6 Turn left at a T-intersection with **Jefferson-Scio Drive**, which eventually becomes **Main Street** in Jefferson.

60.2 Jefferson. Turn right on **Second Street** (former **Highway 99E**).

61.4 Jefferson Middle School. End of ride.

Starting Point: River Park in Lebanon. From U.S. Highway 20 in Lebanon, drive 0.7 mile east on Grant Street, then turn north into the park.

Distance: Long loop — 45.0 miles. Short loop — 34.3 miles.

Terrain: Mainly level, with some hills.

Total Cumulative Elevation Gain: Long loop — 725 feet. Short loop — 675 feet.

Recommended Time of Year: Any season.

Recommended Starting Time: Before 11:00 A.M.

Allow: Long loop — 5 hours. Short loop — 4 hours.

Points of Interest
River Park
Larwood County Covered Bridge and Wayside

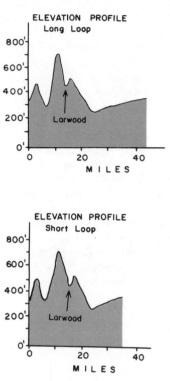

Situated on the South Santiam River, the area surrounding Lebanon is noted for timber and strawberries, two crops at opposite ends of the agricultural spectrum. The routes described below venture up toward the timber-bearing foothills, then return to the flat berry-producing valley of the lower South Santiam River.

Two routes are described. They share a 29-mile section that visits Larwood Bridge, a 1939 covered bridge over Crabtree Creek just a few feet from the mouth of the Roaring River. Linn County has established a perfect little park at the site, an excellent place to enjoy a streamside lunch.

The area north of this ride boasts eight covered bridges, all of which are visited by Trip #31. Several of those bridges can be visited on short detours from this trip.

Only the very first section of these loops is hilly. Eleven miles after leaving

"Stop! It's not a covered bridge!"

Lebanon, the routes cross a shoulder of Mount Hope, reaching an elevation of 700 feet before dropping back down to the 300-foot floor of the valley.

When the routes return to the South Santiam from the foothills, the shorter of the two routes turns south and follows the river back to Lebanon. The longer route continues west, out into the flat berry country, before returning to the river. The longer loop has a couple of short sections of busy road, one of which also involves narrow shoulders. If you choose to ride the longer route, be cautious on these sections.

MILEAGE LOG

LONG LOOP

0.0 River Park in Lebanon. Ride toward the park entrance, then turn left (east) on **Grant Street** and cross a bridge over the South Santiam River (a sidewalk is available on the north side of the bridge).

1.3 Turn right on **Mt. Hope Drive**.

4.1 Shortly after Mt. Hope Drive turns north, continue north on **Bond Road** when Mt. Hope Drive turns east. At mile 5.2, cross Lacomb Drive.

6.5 Turn right on **Baptist Church Drive**.

10.8 Turn left (north) on **Meridian Road** at a T-intersection.

13.7 At a Y-intersection with **Fish Hatchery Drive**, turn right (east).

13.9 Larwood Bridge. Just past the bridge is Larwood County Wayside (day use only; no drinking water), at the junction of Crabtree Creek and the Roaring River. After stopping at the park, recross the bridge and ride west on Fish Hatchery Drive.

14.3 Continue east on Fish Hatchery Drive past the Y-intersection with Meridian Road.

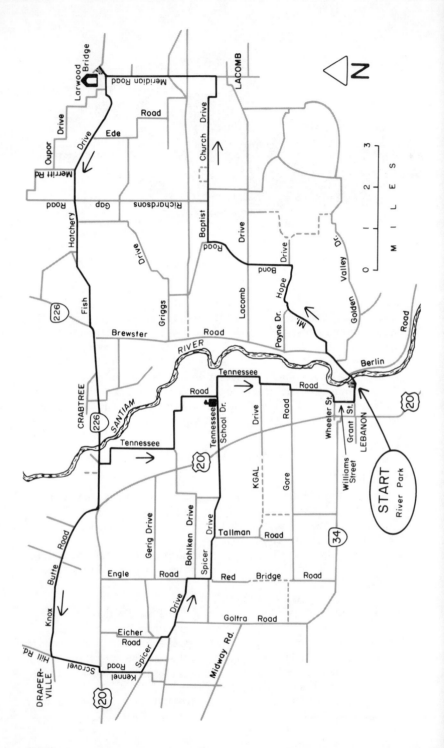

20.9 Turn left on **Highway 226**. At mile 23.9, the highway crosses the South Santiam River. (The short loop turns left on Tennessee Road at mile 24.3.) The shoulder is very narrow from mile 24.3 to mile 25.3; ride carefully.

25.3 Turn right on **Highway 20**.

25.4 Turn right on **Knox Butte Road** (store).

29.6 Draperville. Turn left on **Scravel Hill Road**.

30.8 Turn right on **Highway 20**, then immediately turn left on **Kennel Road**.

31.9 Turn left on **Spicer Drive** and follow it east through several turns and intersections. At mile 38.5, Spicer Drive crosses Highway 20 and becomes **Tennessee School Drive**. After passing Tennessee School at mile 39.8, Tennessee School Drive becomes **Tennessee Road**. The road eventually turns south, then west.

41.6 Turn south, following Tennessee Road, at an intersection with KGAL Drive.

42.5 Turn south, following Tennessee Road, at an intersection with Gore Road. At mile 43.5, Tennessee Road curves right (west) and becomes **Wheeler Street** in Lebanon.

43.9 Turn left on **Williams Street**.

44.4 Turn left on **Grant Street**.

44.9 Turn left at the entrance to River Park.

45.0 River Park. End of ride.

SHORT LOOP

0.0 River Park in Lebanon. Follow the mileage log for the long loop through mile 24.3.

24.3 Turn left on **Tennessee Road**. At mile 26.6, follow Tennessee Road when it turns left (east) at an intersection with Honey Sign Drive.

29.0 Turn left at a T-intersection, following **Tennessee Road**. Tennessee School Drive is on the right. This is mile 39.8 of the long loop. Follow the remainder of the long loop back into Lebanon.

34.3 River Park in Lebanon. End of ride.

Linn County

33 CALAPOOIA RIVER

Starting Point: Periwinkle
School in Albany, at 2200 21st
Avenue (turn east on 21st
Avenue from Geary Street).
Distance: 52.2 miles.
Terrain: Almost all flat.
**Total Cumulative Elevation
Gain:** 450 feet.
Recommended Time of Year:
Any season.
Recommended Starting Time:
10:00 A.M.
Allow: 5 hours.

Points of Interest
Periwinkle Creek Bike Path
Bryant Park
Thompson Rolling Mill
Brownsville
Freeway Lakes Park

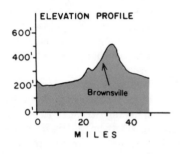

The sleepy little town of Brownsville was once an important trade center for Linn County. But "once" was more than a hundred years ago, when Brownsville was the county seat, the site of a major woolen mill, a Calapooia River ferry crossing, and on the line of the Oregon Railroad.

Today, Brownsville is well off the beaten path. The ferry has been replaced by a steel truss bridge that doesn't seem to go anywhere in particular, the woolen mill burned down, the county seat has moved downstream to Albany, and I-5 is several miles to the west. While other towns have been hurtled into the progress and prosperity of the twentieth century, Brownsville has retained its nineteenth-century character and now boasts one of the most concentrated collections of historic architecture in the state. Brownsville may be off the beaten path, but it's worth beating a path to visit.

The ride starts in Albany, at a modern elementary school, then follows a bike path and downtown streets to Bryant Park at the mouth of the Calapooia River. The route then turns south and crosses flat farmland to Brownsville. This first half of the ride makes nearly two dozen 90-degree turns, and the road names and county road numbers are often confusing. Use the map and mileage log carefully to avoid unexpected detours. A compass will also be helpful. The second half of the ride, on the other hand, has few turns to miss, since much of the route follows Sevenmile Lane due north toward Albany.

Due to the grid nature of the roads between Albany and Brownsville,

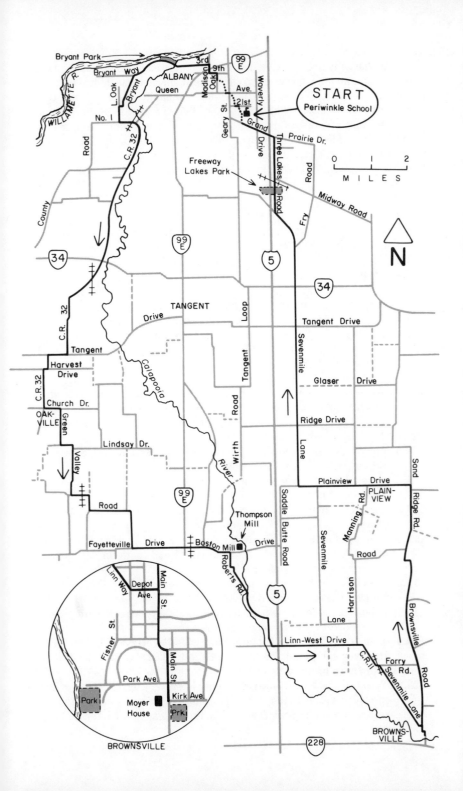

several shortcuts are available to decrease the 50-mile length of the ride. Gravel roads abound, however, so choose your shortcut carefully. One good shortcut crosses the Calapooia near the community of Shedd and then passes the Thompson Rolling Mill, one of two nineteenth-century, water-powered mills still operating in Oregon. The shortcut, which reduces the length of the ride from 52.2 to 37.4 miles, is described in the mileage log.

Even if you don't take the shortcut, the mill is only 0.2 mile off the route, and the picturesque scene of the mill standing next to its millrace is worth a detour.

MILEAGE LOG

0.0 Periwinkle School, on 21st Avenue east of Geary Street in Albany. Ride west on **21st Avenue**.

0.2 Turn right (north) on a **bike path** along Periwinkle Creek.

0.5 At the intersection of the bike path, Geary Street, and Queen Avenue, ride west on the sidewalk on the north side of **Queen Avenue**, then turn north on the **bike path** at mile 0.6.

1.0 When the bike path ends, turn right (north) on **Oak Street**.

1.2 Turn left at a T-intersection with **9th Avenue**.

1.4 Turn right (north) on **Madison Street** and follow it across Pacific Boulevard (Highway 99E).

1.8 Turn left on **3rd Avenue**.

2.7 Follow 3rd Avenue across a bridge over the Calapooia River, after which 3rd Avenue becomes **Bryant Way.** Bryant Park, at the confluence of the Calapooia and Willamette rivers, is on the right at mile 2.8.

3.9 Follow the arterial when it bears left on **Bryant Drive**, leaving Bryant Way (Cherry Lane).

4.8 Follow Bryant Drive when it turns left (south) at an intersection with Lone Oak Lane.

5.3 Turn left (east) at a T-intersection with **County Road 1** (Riverside Drive).

5.9 Turn right on **County Road 32** (Oakville Road). At mile 9.8, carefully cross Highway 34, then follow **Oakville Road** south through several 90-degree turns to Oakville.

14.6 Oakville, which consists primarily of an old church. Turn left on **Church Drive** (County Road 12).

15.1 Follow the arterial as it turns right (south) on **Green Valley Road** and follow it south through several turns.

20.6 Turn left (east) at a T-intersection with **Fayetteville Drive**. Cross Highway 99E at mile 22.0, where Fayetteville Drive becomes **Boston Mill Drive** (County Road 13).

23.3 Turn right on **Roberts Road** (County Road 420). The Thompson Rolling Mill is visible to the east. (For a shortcut, continue straight at this intersection and turn left on Saddle Butte Road at a T-intersection at mile 24.6. At mile 26.7 rejoin the longer route at its mile 41.5, thus reducing the length of the ride by 14.8 miles.)

26.4 Turn left at a T-intersection with **Linn-West Drive** (County Road 26).

28.6 Linn-West Drive joins **Sevenmile Lane**. Follow it as it continues east, then curves to the southeast. It eventually enters Brownsville, where it becomes **Linn Way**.

31.2 Brownsville. Follow the arterial when it bears left on **Depot Avenue**.

31.3 Turn right on **Main Street** and follow it as it turns left, then right, in downtown Brownsville.

31.7 Corner of Main Street and Kirk Avenue. On the left is a small city park (no drinking water), and on the right is the Moyer House (1881), property of the Linn County Historical Society. A second city park (camping permitted, drinking water available) is located at the foot of Park Avenue (turn west one block north of this intersection). After lunch or a break, ride north on **Main Street**, which becomes **Brownsville Road** after leaving Brownsville. At mile 37.3, the name of the road changes to **Sand Ridge Road**.

38.4 Turn left on **Plainview Drive** and pass through Plainview at mile 39.7.

41.5 Follow the arterial as it turns right on **County Road 11** (Sevenmile Lane) and follow it north for several miles.

48.8 Just before an overpass over I-5, turn right on **Three Lakes Road** (Fry Road).

49.3 Freeway Lakes County Park (day use only; water not available).

50.7 Turn left on **Grand Prairie Drive**, then cross I-5 on an overpass.

51.7 About two blocks after passing through an intersection with Waverly Drive, turn right (north) on a **bike path** along Periwinkle Creek.

52.1 Shortly after crossing a bridge over Periwinkle Creek, turn right on a bike path to Periwinkle School.

52.2 Periwinkle School. End of ride.

34 SANTIAM-CALAPOOIA

Starting Point: River Park in Lebanon. From U.S. Highway 20 in Lebanon, drive 0.7 mile east on Grant Street, then turn left into the park.
Distance: 50.3 miles.
Terrain: Mixed flat and hilly.
Total Cumulative Elevation Gain: 1450 feet.
Recommended Time of Year: Any season.
Recommended Starting Time: 10:00 A.M.
Allow: 5 hours.

Points of Interest
River Park
Brownsville
McKercher Park
Crawfordsville Covered Bridge

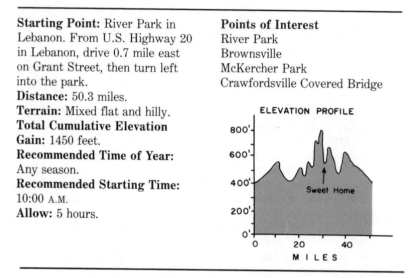

The South Santiam Valley is logging country; the western slopes of the Cascades keep the mills of Lebanon and Sweet Home humming. The area is not noted for fine bicycling, because mountain roads, logging trucks, and bicycles don't usually mix. Bikers can find good routes, however, even in unlikely places like the South Santiam.

This route circles between the South Santiam and Calapooia valleys. Both valleys have enough backroads to make up a loop ride that almost totally avoids the main highways that follow the two rivers. The ride starts in Lebanon, at River Park on the South Santiam, then follows rolling farm roads to Brownsville. Few Oregon towns contain such a concentration of early architecture as does this historic community.

From Brownsville, backroads on the north bank of the Calapooia lead to a 1932 covered bridge at Crawfordsville. Another backroad takes riders on to Holley, after which the South Santiam is reached by crossing a 900-foot pass between Holley and Sweet Home on State Highway 228. The last leg of the ride follows backroads along the east bank of the South Santiam back to Lebanon.

The route is surprisingly level, considering the mountainous country through which it travels. With the exception of the pass between Holley and Sweet Home, the route follows the gentle gradient of the rivers. The level of traffic is low because the route observes an old rule of thumb for bike-route planners: Between any two points, find the main highway that will attract most of the traffic, then follow a backroad that parallels that main highway. On this route, Northern Drive and Crawfordsville Drive

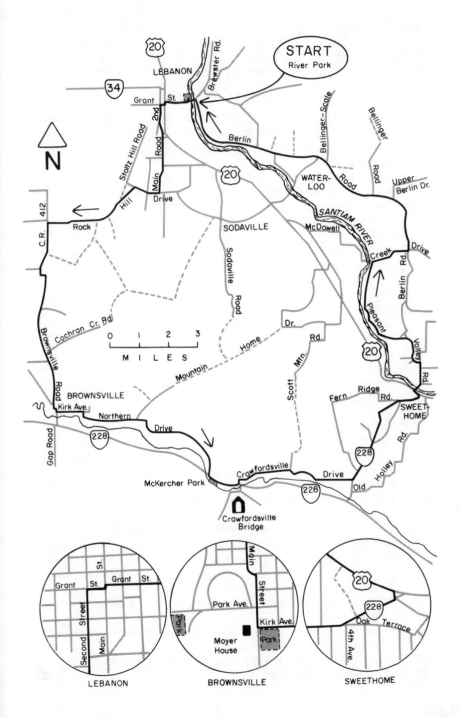

START
River Park

N

LEBANON

Brewster Rd.

20

34

Grant St.

2nd Road

Main Drive

Stoltz Hill Road

Hill

Rock

C.R. 412

Berlin

20

Bellinger-Scale

Bellinger Road

Road

Upper Berlin Dr.

WATER-LOO

SANTIAM RIVER

McDowell

Creek Rd. Drive

SODAVILLE

Sodaville Road

Berlin Rd.

Pleasant

Cochran Cr. Rd.

Brownsville Road

Home

Dr.

Rd.

Mountain

Scott Mtn.

20

Valley Rd.

Fern Ridge Rd.

SWEET-HOME

BROWNSVILLE

Kirk Ave.

Northern Drive

228

Gap Road

Crawfordsville Drive

Old Holley Rd.

228

McKercher Park

Crawfordsville Bridge

0 1 2 3

M I L E S

LEBANON

Grant St. Grant St.

Second Street

Main

Street

St.

BROWNSVILLE

Main Street

Park Ave.

Park

Park

Moyer House

Kirk Ave.

SWEETHOME

20

228

Oak Terrace

4th Ave.

parallel Highway 228 between Brownsville and Holley but have only a fraction of the traffic. Along the South Santiam, Pleasant Valley Road and Berlin Road provide a quiet route from Sweet Home to Lebanon, while all the traffic follows Highway 20 on the opposite bank of the river.

MILEAGE LOG

0.0 River Park at the east end of Grant Street in Lebanon. From the park, ride west on **Grant Street**. At mile 0.8, follow Grant Street when it jogs a few feet south at an intersection with Main Street (Highway 20).

0.9 Turn left (south) on **Second Street**.

1.9 Bear left on **Main Road** and follow it south for two miles.

4.1 Turn right at a T-intersection with **Rock Hill Drive**.

5.1 Follow Rock Hill Drive when it turns left at an intersection with Stoltz Hill Road.

8.7 Turn left at a T-intersection with **County Road 412**. Its name and number will change several times, but follow it south about six miles to Brownsville, where it becomes **Main Street**.

15.1 Brownsville. Follow Main Street when it turns left, then turns right a few feet later. Brownsville has two primitive city parks; one is located on the Calapooia River two blocks west of the route, at the foot of Park Avenue (camping permitted; drinking water available). It can be reached by turning right on Park Avenue at mile 15.2.

15.3 Turn left (east) on **Kirk Avenue**. The second city park is located on the south side of this intersection (day use only; no drinking water).

16.3 Turn right on **Northern Drive**.

22.2 Turn left (east) at a T-intersection with **Highway 228**.

22.4 McKercher Park along the banks of the Calapooia River (day use only; no drinking water).

23.3 Just before a modern bridge over the Calapooia, turn right to a covered bridge that is now closed to auto traffic (Crawfordsville Bridge). After visiting the bridge, cross Highway 228 from the north end of the bridge and ride north and then west on **Crawfordsville Drive**.

27.6 Turn left (north) at a T-intersection with **Highway 228**.

31.5 Sweet Home. Follow Highway 228 when it bears left at an intersection with Fourth Avenue and Oak Terrace.

31.6 Turn left (west) on **Highway 20**, which is a busy four-lane highway. Use the sidewalk on the north side of the highway.

32.0 Turn right on **Pleasant Valley Road** and cross a bridge over the Santiam River.

33.0 Follow Pleasant Valley Road when it turns left (west) at an intersection near Pleasant Valley School.

37.8 Turn right at a T-intersection with **McDowell Creek Drive**.

39.2 Turn left on **Berlin Road**.

50.0 At a T-intersection with **Brewster Road** (unmarked), turn left and cross a bridge over the South Santiam River. A sidewalk is available on the north side of the bridge.

50.3 Turn right into River Park. End of ride.

Linn County

35 HARRISBURG-COBURG HILLS

Starting Point: Harrisburg City Park, at the corner of Fourth and Smith streets, in Harrisburg one block east of State Highway 99E on Smith Street. A public parking lot is located across the intersection from the park.
Distance: 38.0 miles.
Terrain: Generally flat.
Total Cumulative Elevation Gain: 500 feet.
Recommended Time of Year: Any season.
Recommended Starting Time: 11:00 A.M.
Allow: 4 hours.

Point of Interest
Coburg Hills

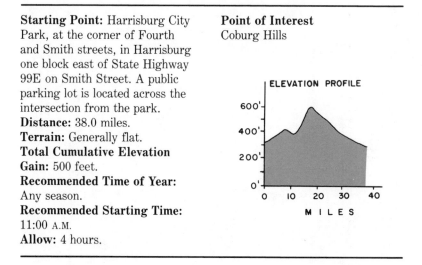

When the first white settlers came to Oregon, they chose their farm sites carefully. Instead of settling along the banks of the Willamette, they chose to settle along the edges of the valley, at the base of the first foothills, where the grasses of the valley met the wooded hillsides. The forests gave them fuel and building materials, while the distance to the river protected them from frequent floods.

The area south of Brownsville is one such place. The line between the flat valley floor and the wooded foothills is distinct. Here the Coburg Hills, a steep 2900-foot ridge, run from the Calapooia River southwest toward Eugene and form a dramatic backdrop to this rectangular route.

From Harrisburg, the route proceeds due east to the base of the ridge, then follows the line between farms and trees north nearly to Brownsville. The third side of the rectangle follows Lake Creek Drive almost to the Willamette, and the fourth side returns to Harrisburg on a six-mile section of the Bikecentennial transcontinental bike route.

As in much of the Willamette Valley, the grid nature of the farm roads

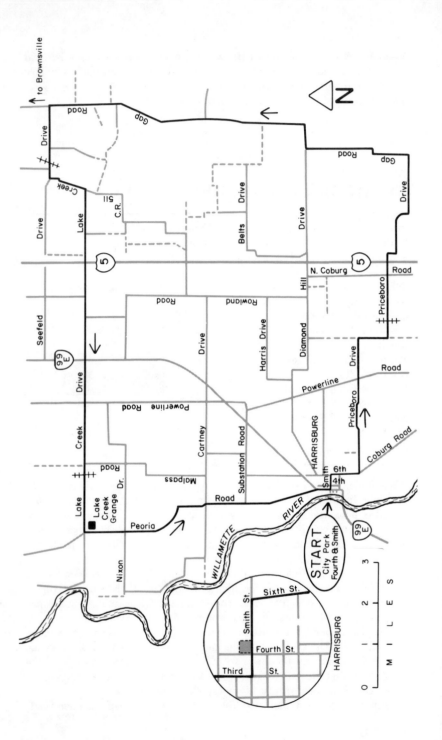

to Brownsville

N

Gap Road

Drive

Creek

Lake

Drive

Seefeld

99 E

C.R. 511

Belts Drive

Drive

Gap Road

Drive

5

5

N. Coburg Road

Hill

Rowland Road

Harris Drive

Diamond

Priceboro

Priceboro Drive

Powerline Road

Drive

Creek

Powerline Road

Cartney

Substation Road

Malpass

Lake Creek Grange

Lake

Dr.

Road

Peoria

Nixon

WILLAMETTE RIVER

HARRISBURG

Smith

6th

4th

START
City Park
Fourth & Smith

99 E

Coburg Road

Smith St.

Sixth St.

Fourth St.

Third St.

HARRISBURG

0   1   2   3

M I L E S

146

here permits numerous shortcuts and variations. Several different roads can be used to cut the rectangle in half, and others can be used to expand the route to the north or south. From the northeast corner of the route, historic Brownsville is only a mile and a half away, although it is not shown on this map. Detours to the west will end on the banks of the Willamette, while detours to the east will be stopped by the Coburg Hills.

MILEAGE LOG

0.0 Harrisburg City Park, at the corner of Fourth and Smith streets in Harrisburg. Ride east on **Smith Street**.

0.2 Turn right (south) on **Sixth Street**. At mile 0.5, cross La Salle Street and continue south on **Sixth Street** (Coburg Road).

1.0 Turn left on **Priceboro Drive** and follow it east for nine miles. At mile 4.4, stay on Priceboro Drive when it turns right (south) at an intersection with a gravel road, and at mile 5.1, follow it left at an intersection with another gravel road. At miles 6.6 and 7.0, Priceboro Drive crosses North Coburg Road and I-5, respectively.

10.0 Priceboro Drive turns left (north) and becomes **Gap Road**.

12.8 T-intersection. Turn right, following Gap Road. At mile 13.5, Gap Road turns north again.

20.1 Turn left on **Lake Creek Drive**.

21.8 Follow Lake Creek Drive as it turns left (south) at an intersection with Seefeld Drive.

22.8 Follow Lake Creek Drive as it turns right (west) at an intersection with County Road 511 (Center School Road). Continue west on Lake Creek Drive for the next 8.5 miles.

31.3 Lake Creek Grange. Turn left (south) on **Peoria Road** and follow it south for 6.3 miles.

37.6 Turn right (south) on **Highway 99E**.

37.9 Harrisburg. Turn left on **Smith Street**.

38.0 Harrisburg City Park at the intersection of Fourth and Smith streets. End of ride.

36 KINGS VALLEY

Starting Point: Aquathusiasts Park in Corvallis at the foot of Tyler Avenue, one block north of the Highway 34 bridges.
Distance: 57.5 miles.
Terrain: Mixed hilly and flat.
Total Cumulative Elevation Gain: 2300 feet.
Recommended Time of Year: Any season.
Recommended Starting Time: 9:00 A.M. or earlier.
Allow: 6 hours.

Points of Interest
Corvallis-Philomath Bike Path
Corvallis riverfront parks
Ritner Wayside and
  Covered Bridge

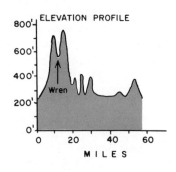

Like many towns that grew up dependent upon the Willamette River for their livelihoods, Corvallis was once centered around a waterfront of warehouses and loading docks serving a busy steamboat trade. Railroads and highways have stolen the river's importance, but Corvallis has found other uses for the Willamette and its tributary Marys River. Both are now lined with parks, boat ramps, and bike paths serving bikers, joggers, and boaters.

This ride explores the countryside northwest of Corvallis. It starts on the town waterfront and follows a scenic bike path from Corvallis to Philomath before striking out for the hillsides and farmland. The bike path follows the west bank of the Willamette and the north bank of the Marys, visiting a half-dozen parks along its seven-mile length.

Unfortunately, the seven miles of the bike path are followed by four miles of U.S. Highway 20, a busy road with no bike lane or path. In fact, the shoulder is nonexistent in places. Riders unaccustomed to narrow roads would do well to try a different ride, or at least get an early start in Corvallis in order to minimize the amount of the traffic on this section.

The rest of the ride makes up for the short section along U.S. Highway 20. The west half of the route follows rolling backroads through wooded valleys, hills planted with trees, and microscopic towns like Wren, Kings Valley, Ritner, Pedee, and Airlie. The east half is flat farmland and visits small communities such as Suver and Lewisburg.

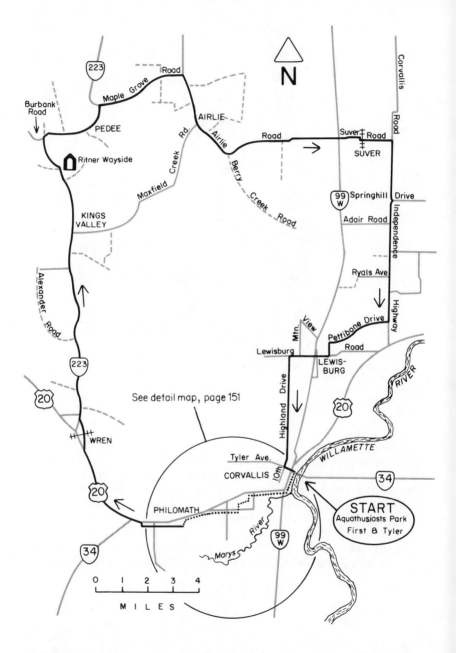

223

Burbank
Road

Maple Grove Road

PEDEE

Ritner Wayside

Maxfield Creek Rd.

AIRLIE

Airlie

Berry Creek Road

Road

Suver Road

SUVER

Corvallis Road

N

99
W Springhill Drive

Adair Road

Independence

KINGS
VALLEY

Ryals Ave

Alexander Road

Pettibone Drive

Highway

223

Mtn. View

Lewisburg Road

LEWIS-
BURG

20

Highland Drive

RIVER

See detail map, page 151

20

WREN

WILLAMETTE

20

Tyler Ave.

CORVALLIS

10th

34

START
Aquathusiasts Park
First & Tyler

34

PHILOMATH

99
W

Marys River

0   1   2   3   4

M I L E S

149

The best place to stop for lunch is inside a covered bridge at Ritner (mile 22.7). When the 1927 bridge was threatened with destruction a few years ago, local residents raised the money to move the bridge a few feet downstream, out of the path of progress. A small wayside park has since been established, complete with picnic tables, one of which is inside the bridge. The bridge is one of only two covered bridges in Polk County; the other is closed to the public.

Just north of Ritner, the hillsides have been taken over by Scotch broom. In late spring, the entire valley seems afire with its yellow bloom.

MILEAGE LOG

0.0 Corner of First Street and Tyler Avenue in Corvallis. Ride south on the bike path along the Willamette River. The bike path will be followed all the way to Philomath. For detail, see map opposite.

0.7 Take either fork in the bike path; the two forks rejoin a short distance later. The path then passes under Highway 99W and proceeds west

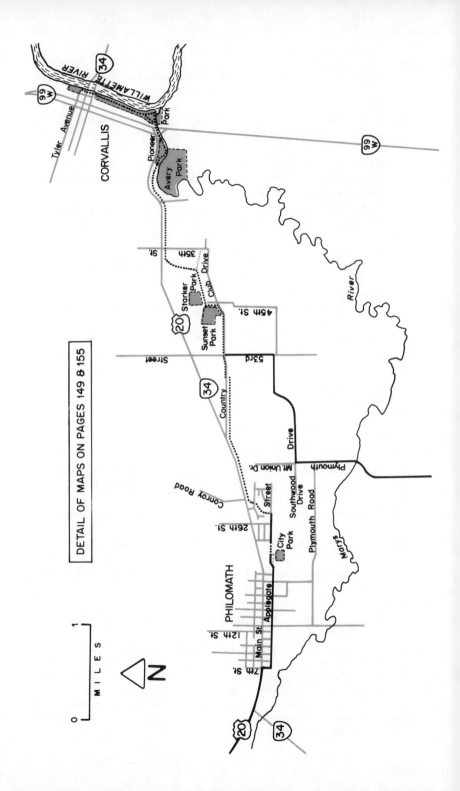

DETAIL OF MAPS ON PAGES 149 & 155

MILES

N

CORVALLIS

WILLAMETTE RIVER

Tyler Avenue

Pioneer Park

Avery Park

35th St.

Starker Park

Club Drive

Sunset Park

45th St.

53rd Street

34

Country

Mt Union Dr.

Southwood Drive

Plymouth Drive

Conroy Road

26th St.

Street

City Park

PHILOMATH

Applegate

Main St.

12th St.

7th St.

Plymouth Road

Mary's River

99W

99W

34

20

20

34

along Marys River through Pioneer Park. Eventually the path parallels Highway 20, then turns south, away from the highway, at mile 2.5.

2.8 Turn right (west) at a Y-intersection in the path. Continue west on the path, disregarding any opportunities to turn right (north).

3.3 At Bruce Starker Arts Park and Sunset Park, the path turns south, then turns east along the shoulder of **Country Club Drive**. At mile 4.6, Country Club Drive joins Highway 20; continue west on the bike path along **Highway 20**.

5.4 Follow the bike path when it turns south, away from the highway, and follows a stream through a residential area.

5.7 Turn right on **Applegate Street**. When it ends, use a bike bridge to continue west to rejoin Applegate, then follow it west through Philomath. A Philomath city park (drinking water available) is located on 23rd Street, a block south of the bike bridge.

7.4 Turn right on **7th Street**.

7.5 Turn left on **Main Street** (Highways 20 and 34). This is a busy road; ride carefully.

7.9 Continue west on Highway 20 when Highway 34 turns south.

11.7 Turn right on an unnamed road with a sign pointing to Wren.

12.3 After passing through Wren, turn right at a T-intersection with **Highway 223** and follow it north for 15 miles.

20.6 Kings Valley (store).

22.7 Ritner Wayside and Covered Bridge.

24.2 Follow Highway 223 when it turns right at an intersection with Burbank Road.

26.4 Pedee.

27.1 When Highway 223 turns left, turn right on **Maple Grove Road**.

30.8 Turn right (south) at a T-intersection with **Airlie Road**.

32.9 Airlie (store).

38.9 Cross Highway 99W (store) and continue east on **Suver Road**.

39.8 Suver.

41.1 Turn right (south) at a T-intersection with **Corvallis Road**, which later becomes Independence Highway. At mile 43.4, bear right (south) on **Independence Highway** at an intersection with Springhill Drive.

48.0 Turn right (west) on **Pettibone Drive**.

51.1 Turn right (west) at a T-intersection with an unmarked road (**Lewisburg Road**).

51.7 Lewisburg (store). Cross 99W and continue west.

52.7 Turn left on **Highland Drive**. Although the road has no shoulder on the right, a wide bike lane is provided on the left. After about two miles, bike lanes are provided on both sides of the road as it enters Corvallis. Eventually, Highland Drive becomes **10th Street**.

57.0 Turn left on **Tyler Avenue**.

57.5 Foot of Tyler Avenue. End of ride.

37 CORVALLIS-HARRISBURG

Starting Point: Aquathusiasts
Park at the foot of Tyler Avenue
in Corvallis, just north of the
Highway 34 bridges.
Distance: 58.2 miles.
Terrain: Flat with some hills.
**Total Cumulative Elevation
Gain:** 1000 feet.
Recommended Time of Year:
Any season.
Recommended Starting Time:
9:00 A.M.
Allow: 6 hours.

Points of Interest
Peoria Park
Lake Creek Mennonite School
William L. Finley National
  Wildlife Refuge
Corvallis-Philomath Bike Path
Corvallis riverfront parks

ELEVATION PROFILE

The east half of this ride is straight and flat; for 22 miles it follows Peoria
Road up the east side of the Willamette from the Corvallis area to Harrisburg. It also happens to be part of the Bikecentennial transcontinental bike
route. The west half, on the opposite side of the Willamette, contrasts
sharply; the roads are serpentine and, in places, hilly.

Nearly 60 miles in length, this ride deserves an early start, particularly in
hot weather, because many of the farm roads are not shaded. Also, no
bridges or ferries cross the Willamette between Corvallis and Harrisburg,
so no shortcuts are available. Riders looking for a shorter route may prefer
to head south from Corvallis for a few miles, then return via the same
route.

On the west side, a good turn-around point may be William L. Finley National Wildlife Area, 15 miles south of Corvallis. The roads within the
refuge itself are gravel, but good views of the refuge are available from the
route, which follows paved Bellfountain Road.

On the east side, Peoria Park, 10 miles south of Corvallis, makes a good
turn-around point, either for a return ride on Peoria Road or for added exploration of the many farm roads east of Peoria. Some of the roads are
shown on this map, and others are shown on the map accompanying Trip
#33 (Calapooia River).

Riders looking for an even longer route can combine either the west half or the east half of this ride with Trip #38 (Eugene-to-Harrisburg) for a one-way ride from Corvallis to Eugene of 40 to 50 miles, or a round trip of about 95 miles.

One interesting feature of the east-side ride is a Mennonite school at mile 16.8. The modest cluster of unadorned white buildings reflects the simple ways of the Mennonites. The Mennonite sect, which includes the Amish church, originated among the Swiss Anabaptists in the 1500s.

MILEAGE LOG

0.0 Aquathusiasts Park in Corvallis, at the foot of Tyler Avenue. Ride south on **First Street** (do not use the bike path on the left side of First). At mile 0.1, cross under the Harrison Boulevard Bridge (west-bound lanes of Highway 34).

0.2 Cross Van Buren Boulevard, then turn left on the bike path/sidewalk on the south side of **Van Buren Boulevard** and cross the bridge over the Willamette (eastbound lane of Highway 34). At the far end of the bridge the bike path ends, but the shoulder is quite adequate.

1.3 Turn right (south) on **Peoria Road**. Follow this road south for 22 miles to Harrisburg. At mile 10.0, Peoria Park (drinking water not available) is on the right, between Peoria Road and the Willamette River. At mile 16.8, the Lake Creek Mennonite School stands on the east side of the road.

23.3 Turn right (south) on **Highway 99E** and follow it through Harris-burg. (Two small city parks are located in Harrisburg. The first is on the Willamette and is reached by riding two blocks west on Monroe Street. The second has drinking water and restrooms and is located one block east of the route on Smith Street.)

23.9 At the south end of Harrisburg, follow Highway 99E as it curves right and crosses a bridge over the Willamette. On the bridge, the sidewalk is the safest route.

24.6 Turn right on **McMullen Lane** and follow it north, then west.

26.1 Turn right at a T-intersection with **Noration Road**. At mile 30.4, continue north on Noration Road through an intersection with Ingram Island Road. At mile 32.5, follow Noration Road north when it turns right (north) at an intersection with Stow Pit Road.

34.1 Turn left (west) on **Hubbard Road**. At mile 35.8, cross Highway 99W, after which Hubbard Road becomes **Dawson Road**.

39.3 Bellfountain (store). Turn right (north) on **Bellfountain Road**. Continue north past the entrance to William L. Finley National Wildlife Refuge at mile 43.3. When Bellfountain Road approaches the Corvallis area, it becomes **Plymouth Drive**.

52.6 Follow Plymouth Drive as it turns 90 degrees right (east) at an intersection with Southwood and Mt. Union drives.

53.9 Turn left (north) at a T-intersection with **53rd Street**.

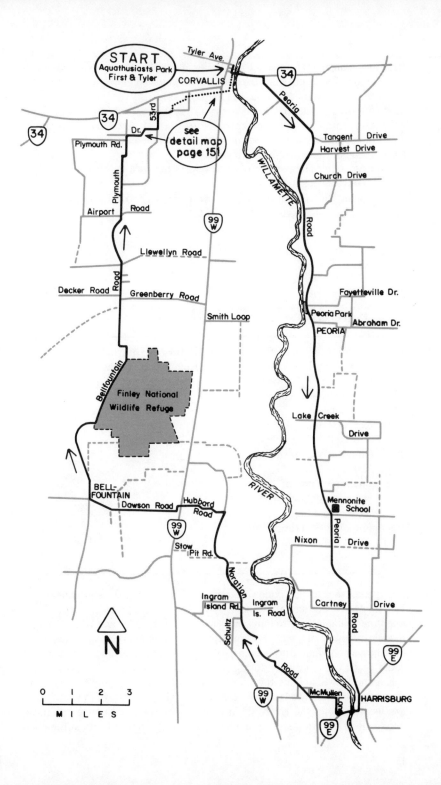

START
Aquathusiasts Park
First & Tyler

Tyler Ave.

CORVALLIS

34

34

34

53rd

Dr.

Plymouth Rd.

see
detail map
page 151

Plymouth

Airport   Road

Road

Llewellyn Road

99
W

Decker Road

Greenberry Road

Smith Loop

Bellfountain

Finley National
Wildlife Refuge

BELL-
FOUNTAIN

Dawson Road   Hubbard
Road

99
W

Stow
Pit Rd.

Naration

Ingram
Island Rd.   Ingram
Is. Road

Schultz

Road

99
W

McMullen

WILLAMETTE

Peoria

Road

Tangent   Drive

Harvest Drive

Church Drive

Fayetteville Dr.

Peoria Park

Abraham Dr.

PEORIA

Lake Creek

Drive

Mennonite
School

Peoria

Nixon   Drive

Cartney   Drive

Road

99
E

HARRISBURG

99
E

RIVER

N

0   1   2   3
MILES

54.4 Turn right on **Country Club Drive**, using the bike path on the north side of the road. This bike path will be followed all the way into downtown Corvallis. See detail map, page 151.

54.7 Follow the bike path as it turns left at the entrance to Sunset Park, then turns right at the entrance to Starker Art Park. Ignore any opportunities to turn left on paths near a small pond.

55.4 Bear left at a fork in the bike path.

57.1 Pass under Highway 99W, then take either fork in the bike path. The two paths rejoin shortly.

58.1 Follow the bike path under the two bridges of Highway 34.

58.2 Foot of Tyler Avenue. End of ride.

Lane County

38 EUGENE-HARRISBURG

Starting Point: Skinner Butte Park parking lot, in Eugene, at the north end of High Street, where High Street becomes Cheshire Avenue.

Distance: 39.9 miles.

Terrain: Flat.

Total Cumulative Elevation Gain: 190 feet.

Recommended Time of Year: Any season, except when the Willamette is flooding.

Recommended Starting Time: 10:00 A.M.

Allow: 4 to 5 hours.

Points of Interest
Eugene bike paths
Armitage State Park

ELEVATION PROFILE

Eugene has probably done a better job of preserving the shoreline of the Willamette River than any other city in the valley. Most other cities have lined the Willamette with industrial sites, but Eugene's river is lined with a model greenway of parks. Perhaps the poor navigability of the Willamette in Eugene contributed to keeping industry off the river; early steamboats could reach the town only during periods of high water.

Eugene may also have the finest system of bike paths and bike lanes in the valley, if not in the Northwest. Not surprisingly, many of the bike paths are located along the river. What is surprising is that Eugene has three bike/pedestrian bridges over the river, equal in number to its automobile

Willamette River bicycle path

bridges. Unfortunately, no other city on the river has a single bike or pedestrian bridge.

The ride starts just a few blocks from downtown Eugene, then follows the river's bike paths. Since the scenery is superb and the paths heavily used by joggers, children, and pets, this is not the place to set speed records.

After four miles of bike paths, the route passes through a two-mile section of commercial development. Although bike lanes are present much of the way, and the traffic only moderate, ride carefully.

After crossing the McKenzie River at Armitage State Park, the volume of traffic drops to almost zero and the horizon is broken only by occasional barns and silos.

The few towns encountered hardly seem to intrude upon the landscape. In Coburg, look for several nineteenth-century houses. One small house along the route is thought to have been built as early as 1848, and another, larger house, built in 1877, is now a well-known restaurant. Farther north, Harrisburg looks like it was lifted off a model railroad set, complete with a water tower proudly painted HARRISBURG.

From Harrisburg, the route crosses the Willamette River and follows Highway 99E south for about two miles, then returns to farm roads. A low point in the road at mile 25.4 is likely to be under water if the Willamette is near flood stage, as it occasionally is during winter or early spring.

Most of the return leg of this trip follows River Road, which was a major thoroughfare prior to the construction of I-5. Most of the evidence of the earlier days is gone, but watch for a faded sign painted on a barn advertising a hotel in Ashland, 210 miles distant.

Shortly after re-entering suburban Eugene, the route returns to the greenway bike paths for the last few miles to Skinner Butte.

MILEAGE LOG

0.0 Parking lot at Skinner Butte Park, at the north end of High Street. From the northwest end of the parking lot, follow a short bike path toward the river, then turn right and follow the bike path southeast along the river. Ignore the many opportunities to turn right, away from the river.

0.3 Pass under the Ferry Street Bridge and continue following the river.

1.3 Turn left and cross the **Autzen Footbridge**. At the north end of the bridge, turn right, then left, and continue following the river upstream (southeast).

1.7 The bike path joins **Day Island Road**. Pass through automobile barriers in the road and continue on Day Island Road at mile 1.9, even though the bike path exits on the right.

2.0 Bear left at an unmarked Y-intersection.

2.1 When the road ends, turn right on a bike path, following a canal.

2.8 Turn left, cross the canal on a footbridge, and proceed north on a bike path along I-5. The path turns left (west) at mile 3.4.

3.5 Turn right (north) and follow a bike path along **Garden Way**. The bike path soon becomes a bike lane.

4.4 Turn right on **Harlow Road**.

4.9 Turn left on **Gateway Street**. This is a busy intersection; use the crosswalks. Follow Gateway Street through a major intersection with Beltline Road, where Gateway Street becomes **Game Farm Road North**.

6.9 Bear right on **Armitage Road**, which grows smaller and smaller, eventually becoming a bike path. The bike path turns right at mile 8.1, passes under I-5, then heads south along I-5.

8.2 Watch for a break in the fence on your left, then turn left into Armitage State Park (camping permitted; water available). Turn left again, then follow the road back under I-5 to the main part of the park. Keep turning left to find the exit from the park to Coburg Road.

8.8 Turn left on **Coburg Road**. Be careful, as Coburg Road is busy in the vicinity of the park. Be particularly careful on the McKenzie River Bridge (mile 9.1), which has neither sidewalks nor shoulders. Either wait for a lull in the traffic or, if necessary, claim the center of the lane to prevent cars from passing on the bridge.

11.0 Coburg. Follow the arterial through the town, as Coburg Road

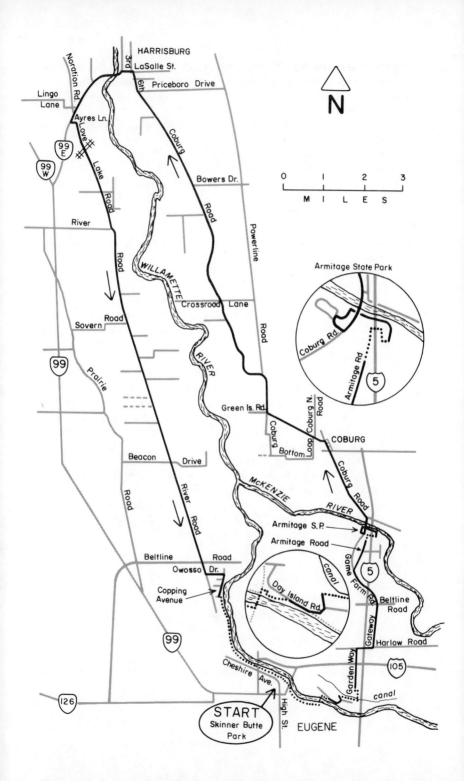

becomes **Willamette Street**, turns west on **Van Duyn Street**, then regains the name **Coburg Road**. The Van Duyn-Van Massey House (ca. 1848-1850) at 238 W. Van Duyn Street may be the oldest building in the county.

11.5 Continue west on Coburg Road; do not turn right on Coburg North Road.

12.8 Follow Coburg Road as it turns right at an intersection with Green Island Road and Coburg Bottom Loop.

13.8 Stay on Coburg Road when it turns left at an intersection with Powerline Road. At mile 21.7, Coburg Road enters Harrisburg and becomes **Sixth Street**.

22.2 Turn left on **LaSalle Street**.

22.5 Turn left on **Third Street** (Highway 99E). At mile 22.6, the highway crosses the Willamette River. On the bridge, use of the sidewalk is recommended because it continues for about a half mile past the bridge, and the shoulder is narrow. After leaving the sidewalk, Highway 99E is fairly busy, and the shoulder bumpy. Exercise care.

24.5 Turn left on **Ayres Lane**. At mile 24.7, Ayres Lane turns south and becomes **Love Lake Road**. At mile 25.4, the road passes under two very low railroad trestles. If the Willamette is flooding, beware of high water here.

27.3 Turn left on **River Road** and follow it all the way into Eugene. At mile 33.2, a bike lane starts on the right side of the road and a bike path appears from time to time. Since traffic picks up in this area, the bike path is the best choice when available. After passing under Beltline Road at mile 35.8, watch for Owosso Drive on the left.

36.2 Turn left on **Owosso Drive**.

36.5 Turn right on **Copping Avenue** and follow it south.

36.9 Copping Avenue ends and a bike path starts. Follow the bike path as it turns left toward the river, then proceeds south along the river. Follow the river, ignoring various bike paths that turn right, away from the river. At mile 38.5, continue past a footbridge on the left over the river. After passing Skinner Butte at about mile 39, watch for the parking lot on the right.

39.9 Turn right to the parking lot. End of trip.

39 LOWER LONG TOM

Starting Point: Kirk Park, on Clear Lake Road at the western end of Fern Ridge Dam, 10 miles northwest of Eugene.
Distance: 48.1 miles.
Terrain: Generally flat with some moderate hills.
Total Cumulative Elevation Gain: 800 feet.
Recommended Time of Year: Any season, except during periods of flooding.
Recommended Starting Time: 10:00 A.M.
Allow: 5 hours.

Points of Interest
Fern Ridge Lake
Kirk Park
Richardson Park
Monroe City Park
Orchard Point Park

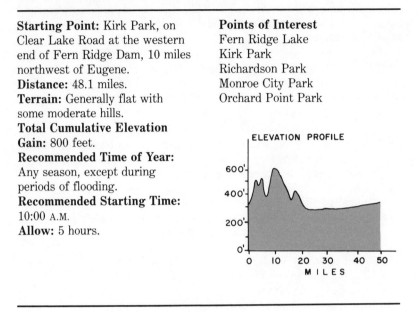

The Long Tom River drains the foothills of the Coast Range northwest of Eugene and joins the Willamette near the town of Monroe. In the late 1930s, the Long Tom was dammed near Alvadore, creating a huge, nine-thousand acre reservoir, Fern Ridge Lake. This ride starts near the dam spillway and circles the lower valley of the Long Tom.

The western half of the route climbs up and down the foothills of the Coast Range, while the eastern half cruises flat farm roads along the Willamette. Most of the roads are quite narrow but have little traffic to distract from the pastoral surroundings.

Although the route is nearly 50 miles in length, the general grid pattern of the farm roads permits several shorter rides to be taken within the 50-mile loop. For example, High Pass Road splits the loop roughly in half horizontally at Junction City. By turning east, rather than west, at mile 10.7 and following High Pass Road to River Road at mile 33.7 of the regular route, the total length of the ride can be reduced to about 32 miles.

For those wishing to avoid the hills on the western part of the ride, a right turn on Applegate Trail Road at mile 4.7 will give access to Territorial Highway near Cheshire, which joins the regular route at mile 16.9.

The Fern Ridge and Long Tom area offer superb bird watching. Depending on the season, the area around the small lake near Kirk Park may host a variety of hawks and owls, as well as gulls, ducks, and other shorebirds. In winter, the area near Amazon Creek north of mile 42 is home to hundreds of whistling swans.

If the winter has been particularly wet and the Willamette is near flood stage, one section of the ride at mile 31.2 will be impassable due to several feet of water on the road. Either wait for drier weather or work out a shorter loop to avoid the section.

Winter is also the least scenic time to view the reservoir, since the water level is lowered in late autumn each year to make room for winter's rains. The water level is usually back to normal by late spring, when the lake becomes a sailing and water-skiing mecca for Eugene residents.

MILEAGE LOG

0.0 Kirk Park. Leave the parking lot, turn right on **Clear Lake Road**, and cross the bridge over the reservoir outlet (the Long Tom River). The entrance to Richardson Park is on the left at mile 1.3.

1.5 Bear right, following Clear Lake Road, at an intersection marked by a sign pointing left to the Eugene Yacht Club.

1.6 Intersection with **Territorial Road** (unmarked). Turn right (north). At mile 4.7, follow Territorial Road as it bears left at the community of Franklin.

6.3 Turn right at a T-intersection with **Highway 36**.

6.4 Turn left on **Valley View Road** (Allen-Bales Road).

6.7 Turn left on **Hall Road**.

8.1 Turn right on **Smyth Road**.

10.7 T-intersection with **High Pass Road**. Turn left (west).

12.4 Turn right on **Turnbow Road**.

14.0 T-intersection with **Ferguson Road**. Turn right.

16.9 Turn left on **Territorial Road** and follow it north to Monroe.

21.4 Monroe. Turn right on **Highway 99W** and cross the Long Tom River. Monroe City Park is on the left at mile 21.6.

21.9 Turn left on **Ingram Island Road**.

24.1 T-intersection with **Noration Road** (unmarked). Turn right (south).

24.3 Bear right at a Y-intersection, following Noration Road. The left fork is Ingram Island Road.

30.0 Noration Road joins Highway 99E at the community of Lancaster (store). Turn right (south) on **Highway 99E**.

30.2 Turn left on **Ayres Lane**. At mile 30.4, Ayres Lane turns south and becomes **Love Lake Road**. At mile 31.2, the road dips under two very low railroad trestles. If the Willamette is near flood stage, this section of the road will be under several feet of water.

33.0 Turn left (south) on **River Road**.

35.4 Turn right on **Severn Road**.

37.0 T-intersection with **Prairie Road**. Turn left (south).

39.3 Turn right on **Meadowview Road**. At mile 40.5, cross Highway 99.

43.5 Turn left (south) at an unmarked T-intersection with **Alvadore Road**.

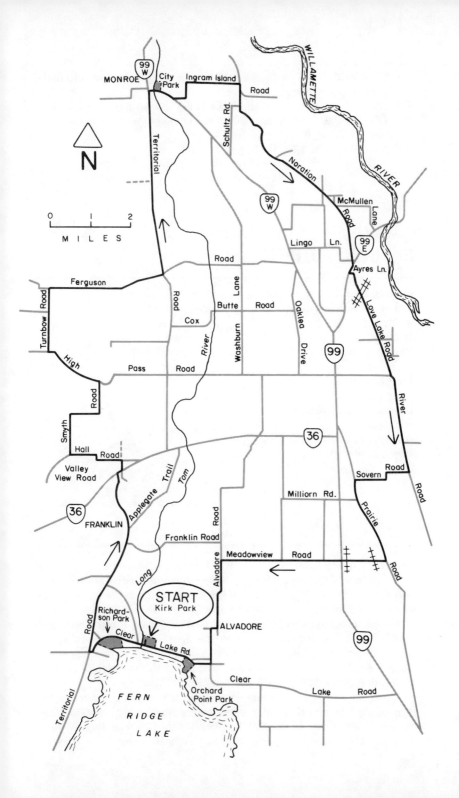

At mile 45.3, stay on Alvadore Road as it turns right, then left, in the small town of Alvadore (store).

46.2 Store. Turn right on **Clear Lake Road** (unmarked). At mile 46.7, Orchard Point Park is on the left, and Orchard Point Marina is on the left at mile 47.0.

48.1 Turn right into Kirk Park. End of ride.

Lane County

40 FERN RIDGE

Starting Point: Echo Hollow Pool at 1655 Echo Hollow Road in Eugene.
Distance: 32.8 miles.
Terrain: Rolling farmland with one moderate hill.
Total Cumulative Elevation Gain: 700 feet.
Recommended Time of Year: Any season.
Recommended Starting Time: Before 11:00 A.M.
Allow: 4 hours.

Points of Interest
Orchard Point Park
Fern Ridge Lake
Kirk Park
Richardson Park

ELEVATION PROFILE

West of Eugene, where the Long Tom River once flowed through a broad valley, lies one of the largest lakes in western Oregon. Created by the Army Corps of Engineers in 1941 when Fern Ridge Dam was completed, Fern Ridge Lake is nearly five miles long and five miles wide.

The lake is surrounded by farms, oak and evergreen forests, and small towns like Elmira, Veneta, and Crow. This 33-mile ride starts on the west side of Eugene and follows backroads around the reservoir and into the foothills south of it. The ride is a gentle one, with the only significant hill a moderate one over a pass between Veneta and Crow.

During the summer, when the water level in Fern Ridge Lake is at its highest, the lake is very popular for swimming and boating, especially sailing and water skiing. As a result, the section of the ride from Eugene out to the parks at the north end of the lake may be heavily trafficked. Once the

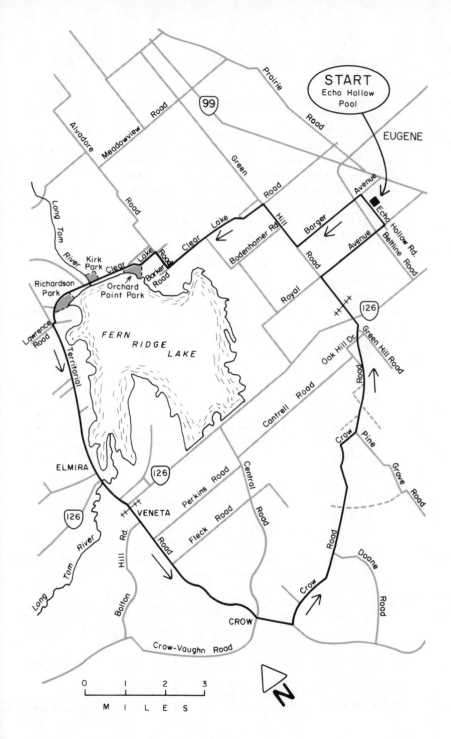

west side of the lake is reached, however, the roads should be free of most motor vehicles.

The ride starts and ends in suburban west Eugene. The first and last few miles are on busy arterials, but, as is typical for Eugene, bike lanes are provided.

Throughout the year, Fern Ridge Lake is a prime habitat for birds. Even if you're not normally interested in bird watching, some of the larger species will be hard to miss. Great blue herons, whistling swans, and turkey vultures are common, and less abundant species include osprey and several types of hawks and owls. The two most frequently seen hawks are the marsh hawk (a dark bird with a white rump) and the red-tailed hawk. Take your binoculars along, particularly in winter when many of the birds keep their distance across the expansive mudflats.

MILEAGE LOG

0.0 Echo Hollow Pool in Eugene. Leave the parking lot and ride north on **Echo Hollow Road**, using the bike lane.

0.3 Turn left on **Barger Avenue** and follow it west out into the country.

2.4 Turn right at a T-intersection with **Green Hill Road**.

3.6 Turn left at an intersection with **Clear Lake Road**.

6.4 Follow Clear Lake Road as it turns right (north) at an intersection with Barker Road.

6.9 Follow Clear Lake Road (Snyder Road) when it turns left (west) at an intersection with Alvadore Road (store). At mile 7.4, Orchard Point Park is on the left, then at mile 7.7, Fern Ridge Lake becomes visible to the left. The road traverses the length of the dam, then at mile 8.8, the entrance to Kirk Park is on the right just before the road passes in front of the spillway. The entrance to Richardson Park is on the left at mile 10.0.

10.3 At an intersection of Clear Lake Road, Lawrence Road, and Territorial Road, turn left on **Territorial Road** (unmarked) and follow it south for several miles. Pass through the town of Elmira at mile 14.0 and cross the Long Tom River at mile 14.3. At mile 15.3, pass through the town of Veneta. Between Elmira and Veneta, Territorial Road is part of Highway 126. At mile 18.0, the road begins to climb into the hills south of the reservoir, reaching a crest at mile 19.0.

19.7 Crow (store). Continue south on Territorial Road.

20.6 Turn left on **Crow Road** and follow it northeast for several miles. At mile 28.6, continue north through an intersection with Oak Hill Drive. At this point, Crow Road becomes **Green Hill Road.** Cross Highway 126 at mile 28.8.

30.1 Turn right on **Royal Avenue**. At mile 31.3, bike lanes start on both sides of Royal.

32.1 Turn left on **Echo Hollow Road**.

32.8 Turn right into the parking lot at Echo Hollow Pool. End of ride.

41 LORANE LOOPS

Starting Point: Acorn Park, at the intersection of West 15th Avenue and Buck Street in Eugene. Park along Buck Street on the west side of the park.
Distance: Long loop — 64.4 miles. Short loop — 34.6 miles.
Terrain: Hilly.
Total Cumulative Elevation Gain: Long loop — 2780 feet. Short loop — 1385 feet.
Recommended Time of Year: Any season.
Recommended Starting Time: Long loop — Before 9:00 A.M. Short loop — 11:00 A.M.
Allow: Long loop — 7 hours. Short loop — 4 hours.
Points of Interest
Siuslaw River
Siuslaw Falls Park

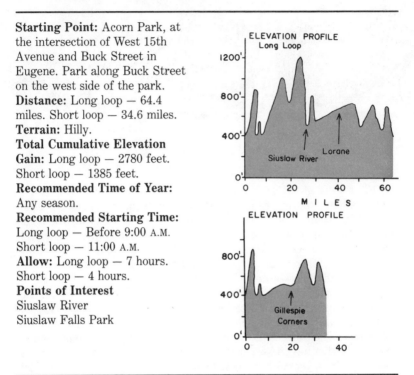

The flat Willamette Valley ends at Eugene, where the main stem of the Willamette is formed by the meeting of the Coast Fork, the Middle Fork, and the McKenzie rivers. These three tributaries join the Willamette from the south and east and provide relatively easy access into the Cascades.

For travellers headed into the Coast Range southwest from Eugene, however, no such broad valleys are available. Instead, a series of high ridges and small, but deep, stream valleys separate the Eugene area from the Siuslaw and Umpqua valleys.

This route climbs up and down these ridges on its way to visit the Siuslaw River. It starts in west Eugene, near Amazon Creek, climbs over Murray Hill, then follows Coyote Creek to the Crow area. From near Crow, the route climbs to a 1000-foot pass before dropping to Wolf Creek, which is followed by another climb to a 1200-foot pass and a steep descent to the Siuslaw River. After following the Siuslaw River to the tiny town of Lorane, the route returns to Coyote Creek, then climbs over one more pass before returning to suburban Eugene.

"Here, Birdy! Here, Birdy!"

The southern section of the route, especially the descent to, and the ride along, the Siuslaw River, is one of the nicest rides in the state. The roads, while narrow, are shady, secluded, smooth, and free of traffic. Particularly when dropping down to the river, the endless curves through the woods are a joy. An autumn ride, after the foliage has turned color, is superb.

Although the full loop to the Siuslaw and back to Eugene is nearly 65 miles, the scenery makes it well worthwhile. If 65 miles is outside of your range, you may take the shorter loop of 35 miles, but it returns to Eugene well before the Siuslaw is reached. To see the Siuslaw in a shorter trip, the long loop can be converted to a manageable 43.6-mile loop by starting, for example, in Lorane and using the map and mileage log to ride north to Gillespie Corner, northwest toward Crow, then southwest to the Siuslaw River, which can then be followed back to Lorane.

This ride can also be used as a scenic, but hilly, backroads route to the coast by turning west on Siuslaw River Road at mile 26.0 and following it along the river, eventually reaching Florence via State Highway 126.

MILEAGE LOG

LONG LOOP

0.0 Acorn Park in Eugene. Ride south on **Buck Street**.

0.2 Turn right on **18th Avenue** and follow its bike lane west. At mile 1.4, the bike lane ends at an intersection with Bertelson Road. Continue west on 18th Avenue.

2.2 Turn left on **Willow Creek Road** (Williams Street). At mile 2.5, the road turns west and becomes **25th Avenue** but later regains the name **Willow Creek Road**. The road climbs steadily up the side of Murray Hill. At mile 4.3, the road reaches its high point of 880 feet, then turns north and becomes **Green Hill Road**.

5.7 Turn left at a T-intersection with **Crow Road** on the left and Green Hill Road on the right. The road climbs over a gentle pass, then

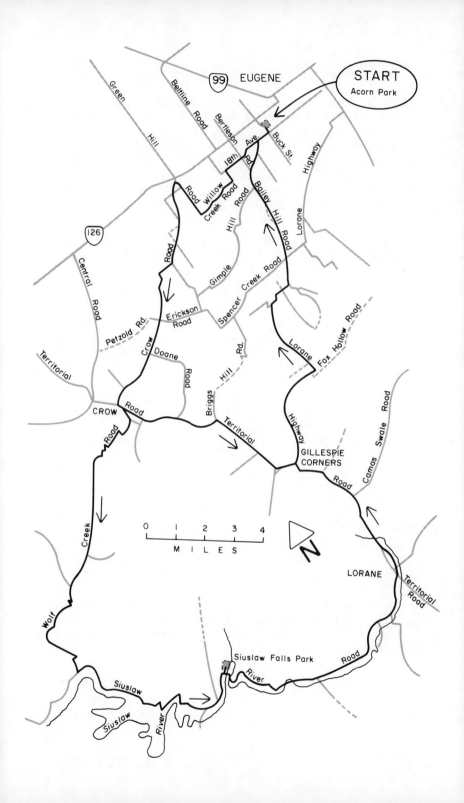

enters a valley of flat farmland as it follows Coyote Creek toward the town of Crow.

13.9 Turn left at a T-intersection with **Territorial Road** (unmarked).

14.2 Turn right on **Wolf Creek Road**. (The short loop, which is described below, goes straight here.) Wolf Creek Road climbs to 1010 feet at mile 16.7, then drops into the Wolf Creek Valley. Another climb brings the rider to a 1200-foot pass, after which the road becomes quite narrow as it drops to the Siuslaw River.

26.0 Turn left at a T-intersection with **Siuslaw River Road** and follow it east up the river. Although the gradient of the river is not steep, the road climbs up and down several small ridges.

34.9 Turn left at a sign pointing to Siuslaw Falls Park.

35.3 Siuslaw Falls Park (picnic facilities). Return to Siuslaw River Road.

35.7 Turn left on **Siuslaw River Road**. Beyond this point the road is fairly gentle.

44.8 Lorane (store). Go straight on **Territorial Road**, which soon curves north.

50.9 Gillespie Corners. Turn right (northeast) on **Lorane Highway**. (The short loop rejoins the long loop at this intersection.) Lorane Highway proceeds east and north along a stream known simply as Fox Hollow. At mile 54.6, Lorane Highway turns due north and climbs over a small pass into the Spencer Creek Valley.

59.5 Intersection with Spencer Creek Road. Although Lorane Highway turns right here, continue straight (north) on **Bailey Hill Road**, which climbs to a 740-foot pass at mile 61.1.

62.6 Bear right at a Y-intersection with **Bertelson Road**. A bike lane is available on the right.

63.7 Turn right on **18th Avenue**.

64.2 Turn left on **Buck Street**.

64.4 Acorn Park. End of ride.

SHORT LOOP

0.0 Acorn Park. Follow the mileage log for the long loop to mile 14.2.

14.2 Do not turn on Wolf Creek Road, but continue straight (southeast) on Territorial Road and follow it as it continues up the Coyote Creek Valley.

21.1 Gillespie Corners. Although Territorial Road turns right (south), turn east on **Lorane Highway**. This intersection is mile 50.9 of the long loop. To return to Eugene, follow the mileage log for the long loop.

34.6 Acorn Park. End of ride.

42 MIDDLE FORK

Starting Point: Tyson Park, at the corner of 34th and E streets in Springfield. Park along the south side of E Street.

Distance: 39.0 miles.

Terrain: Relatively flat; some hills.

Total Cumulative Elevation Gain: 775 feet.

Recommended Time of Year: Any season.

Recommended Starting Time: 10:00 A.M.

Allow: 4 to 5 hours.

Points of Interest
Four covered bridges
Dexter Reservoir
Dexter Park
Jasper Park

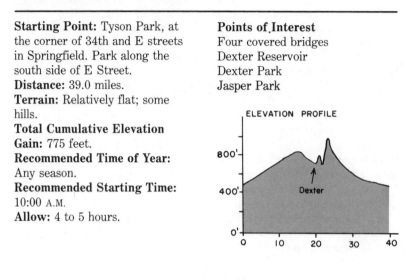

The Middle Fork of the Willamette River flows from the crest of the Cascades south of Willamette Pass to the Eugene/Springfield area, where it joins the Coast Fork. It drains an area of dense forests, small logging towns, and a few small farms. Its valley is home to a number of covered bridges.

Only two major roads enter the valley from the west. State Highway 58 is the main thoroughfare, leading out of Eugene over Willamette Pass. The other highway is Jasper Road, which starts in Springfield and winds its way along the river, joining Highway 58 at Dexter Reservoir. This ride spends much of its time on little-travelled Jasper Road and follows Highway 58 only as necessary to visit all four of the remaining covered bridges of the lower valley.

The bridges are located at Pengra, Unity, Lowell, and Dexter. The Pengra bridge, built in 1938, contains 126-foot timbers in its floor and 98-foot timbers in its roof. The Unity bridge, the only one of the four still open to automobile traffic, includes a full-length window on the upstream side.

The Lowell bridge was built in 1945 to replace an older covered bridge damaged by an errant truck. Although one of the youngest covered bridges in the state, it surely must have nine lives. In 1953, when Dexter Dam and Reservoir were built and the area flooded, a causeway was built across the reservoir and the bridge raised several feet to accommodate the higher waters. Then, when heavy logging-truck traffic necessitated a modern structure, the bridge was moved to one side and given a well-deserved retirement, although it is still open to pedestrians and bicyclists.

The last bridge, at Parvin, was similarly preserved for pedestrian and bicycle use when Rattlesnake Road was realigned and a new bridge built a quarter of a mile downstream. In the last 30 years, apparently only one covered bridge in this area has been destroyed: the bridge at Fall Creek, replaced by a concrete structure. Perhaps the remaining four can be preserved indefinitely.

The ride starts in Springfield, at a suburban park, then follows Jasper Road up the Middle Fork. Although not heavily travelled, Jasper Road has a moderate amount of traffic and narrow shoulders. In a few places, the shoulder is nonexistent.

After passing through Jasper, the road follows Fall Creek past two covered bridges, then climbs over a small ridge to Dexter Reservoir and the town of Lowell. The ride crosses the reservoir and follows Highway 58 for two miles. Although Highway 58 is quite busy, the shoulder is adequate. Even so, ride with care, and minimize the time you spend on this section.

The last covered bridge is visited south of the reservoir, in the Lost Creek Valley. After a climb over an intervening ridge, the route passes through flat farmland, then returns to Jasper and Springfield.

MILEAGE LOG

0.0 Tyson Park, at the corner of 34th and E streets in Springfield. Ride east on **E Street**, then turn south and cross the middle of the park on a bike path.

0.1 Leave the park and continue south on **35th Street**. Cross Main Street (Highway 126) at mile 0.4.

0.7 Turn right on **Virginia Street**.

0.9 Turn left on **32nd Street** at a T-intersection. At mile 1.4, 32nd turns left (east) and becomes **Jasper Road**. Follow Jasper Road for the next nine miles, up the Middle Fork of the Willamette River, through the town of Jasper at mile 6.8.

10.7 Just before a bridge over the Middle Fork, turn left on **Jasper-Lowell Road**.

11.0 Turn right on **Place Road**, to Pengra Bridge, then return to **Jasper-Lowell Road** and turn right.

13.3 Fall Creek. Turn right, following Jasper-Lowell Road across Little Fall Creek.

15.8 Unity (store). Pass through Unity Bridge, then continue straight on Jasper-Lowell Road.

17.6 Lowell. Ride straight through the major intersection with Pengra Road, then turn left on the next street (Main Street; unmarked).

18.0 Turn right on the next available street (Pioneer Street; unmarked). Lowell High School is on the southwest corner of this intersection. The road proceeds south, out of Lowell, and across Dexter Reservoir

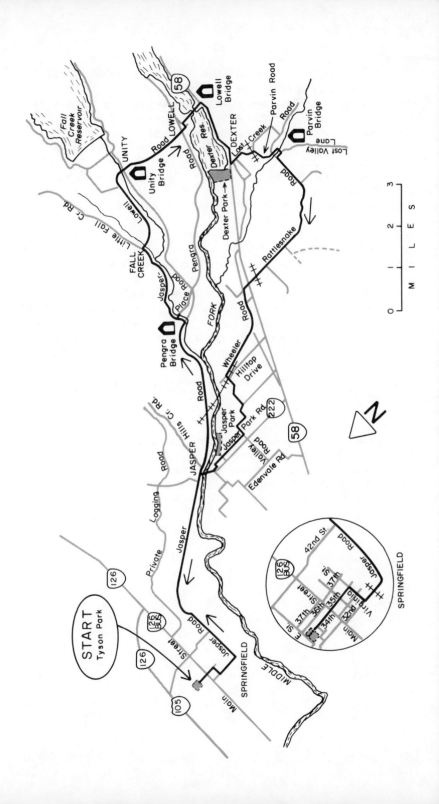

on a causeway. At the far end of the causeway, Lowell Bridge stands on the right side of the road, no longer in use.

18.7 Turn right at a T-intersection with **Highway 58**, being careful of the moderate to heavy traffic on this main highway.

20.5 Turn left, onto **Lost Creek Road**, at the signs pointing to Dexter. Dexter Park (drinking water available; camping permitted) is located north of this intersection.

21.2 Immediately after passing under a railroad bridge, turn right on **Parvin Road**.

21.8 At an intersection with Rattlesnake Road, go straight, despite a deadend sign.

22.0 Parvin Bridge. Cross the bridge, then turn right on **Lost Valley Lane**.

22.2 Turn left at a T-intersection with **Rattlesnake Road**.

26.2 Cross Highway 58.

26.4 Turn left at a T-intersection with **Wheeler Road**.

28.8 Follow Wheeler Road when it turns left and passes under a railroad bridge. Stay on Wheeler Road as it works its way west and north.

30.6 Turn right on **Jasper Park Road**, one block before a stop sign. At mile 31.4, Jasper Park is on the right. At mile 31.7, Jasper Park Road turns left, then right to join Highway 222.

31.9 Turn right on **Highway 222** and cross the Middle Fork on a large bridge.

32.1 Jasper. Turn left on **Jasper Road** and follow it downstream, retracing the route from Springfield.

37.5 Jasper Road turns north and becomes **32nd Street**.

37.9 Turn right on **Virginia Street**.

38.2 Turn left on **35th Street** and follow it to its end.

38.8 Cross Tyson Park, then turn left on **E Street**.

39.0 Corner of 34th and E streets. End of ride.

43 SCAPONIA

Starting Point: West Union School, 12 miles west of Portland. From U.S. Highway 26, turn north on Helvetia Road and drive one mile, then turn west on West Union Road.
Distance: 94.6 miles.
Terrain: Extremely hilly with some flat sections.
Total Cumulative Elevation Gain: 3800 feet.
Recommended Time of Year: Any season, except during periods of snowfall at elevations of 1000 feet or less.
Recommended Starting Time: 6:00 A.M. if ridden in one day.
Allow: 1 or 2 days.

Points of Interest
Verboort
Nehalem Valley
Columbia County Historical
  Society Museum
Scaponia Recreation Area
Bonnie Falls

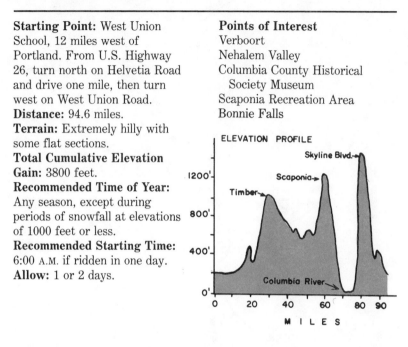

ELEVATION PROFILE

The Nehalem River carves a hundred-mile arc across the north end of Oregon's Coast Range. From its source near the small town of Timber in Washington County, the river flows north through Columbia County before turning west and south to the Pacific. Its deep, wooded valley is sparsely populated, and the single road that follows the river has little traffic.

This ride, also nearly a hundred miles in length, starts in the Tualatin Valley, climbs over a thousand-foot pass to join the Nehalem at Timber, then follows the river through the town of Vernonia. A few miles north of Vernonia, the route turns east, away from the Nehalem, and climbs to 1200 feet before dropping to the town of Scappoose on the Columbia. After an all too brief level section along the Columbia, the route returns to the hills by ascending Rocky Point Road. In 3.3 excruciating miles, the road climbs from the Columbia to Skyline Boulevard on the 1475-foot crest of the Tualatin Mountains. The effort to ride it does not go unrewarded, however, for the last leg of the journey is a long descent into the Tualatin Valley.

The 95-mile distance and the 3800-foot cumulative elevation gain combine to make this an extremely rigorous ride for even the best of riders. Some riders will be able to complete the route in a single day, but most will

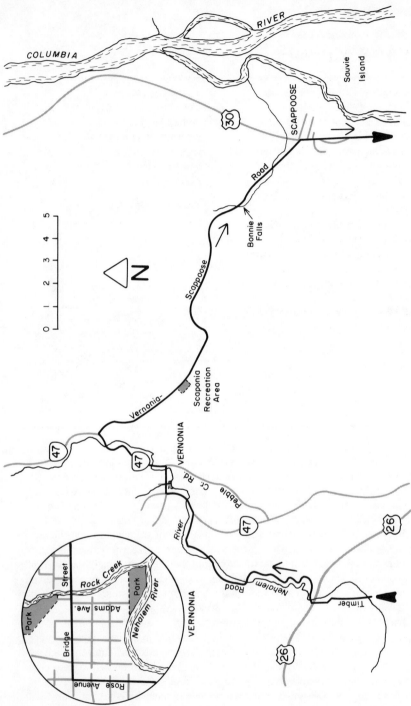

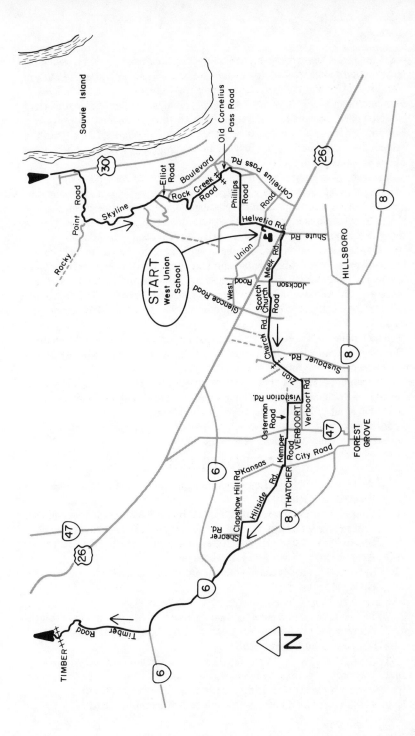

177

want to spread the work over two days. Public campgrounds are available at two points along the route. At mile 44.5, Anderson Park, a city park in Vernonia, offers pleasant camping along the Nehalem River. At mile 57.6, Scaponia Recreation Area, a BLM campground, straddles the East Fork of the Nehalem. Obviously named for the two towns between which it lies, Scaponia is one of the prettiest campgrounds around. Hiking trails, a secluded location, and rustic bridges over a gurgling stream all add up to make Scaponia a fine place to camp.

A ride of this length and terrain requires a fit rider and a degree of careful planning. A one-day ride frees you from carrying heavy overnight gear, but a hundred-mile ride over steep hills should not be attempted by riders unsure of their stamina. Try several shorter rides first, then get a favorable weather forecast and an early start on the chosen day.

A two-day ride, although burdened with luggage, gives a much more leisurely pace, permitting sightseeing and exploring along the way. Stop in Verboort, a little town of Dutch ancestry, famous for its annual sausage festival. Centered around the Visitation Catholic Church (1875), Verboort is a strongly religious community; don't expect any stores to be open on Sunday.

Even smaller is Timber, in the Coast Range at the head of the Nehalem. The road literally switchbacks its way through this tiny logging town, which seems to be glued to the steep hillside.

In Vernonia, a two-day ride will permit leisurely stops at two city parks located on Rock Creek and the Nehalem River, or it will allow a visit to the Columbia County Historical Society Museum.

Most important of all, a two-day ride permits frequent stops to catch one's breath while climbing the long hills.

MILEAGE LOG

0.0 West Union School. Leave the parking lot and turn right (east) on **West Union Road**.

0.1 Bear right at an intersection with **Helvetia Road** and follow it south.

1.0 Carefully cross Highway 26, after which Helvetia Road becomes **Shute Road**. (In 1984, this intersection was scheduled to be reconstructed into a two-level interchange.)

1.1 Turn right on **Meek Road** and follow it as it bears right, then parallels Highway 26.

3.6 Turn right at a T-intersection with **Jackson Road**.

3.7 Turn left (west) on **Scotch Church Road**. After passing through an intersection with Glencoe Road at mile 5.4, Scotch Church Road becomes **Zion Church Road**.

9.2 At a T-intersection, turn right (west) on **Verboort Road**.

10.2 Verboort. Turn right on **Visitation Road**.

11.1 Turn left (west) at a T-intersection with **Osterman Road**.

12.0 Cross Highway 47 and continue west on **Kemper Road**.

13.8 Thatcher. Turn right (north) on **Kansas City Road**.

13.9 Turn left on **Hillside Road**.

17.4 Turn left (west) at a T-intersection with **Clapshaw Hill Road**. At mile 17.9, continue west on Clapshaw Hill Road through an intersection with Shearer Road, after which Clapshaw Hill Road drops rapidly into the Gales Creek Valley.

18.8 Turn right on **Highway 8** (Gales Creek Road).

20.7 Turn left on **Highway 6**, which has a moderate amount of traffic. Ride carefully.

24.1 Turn right (north) at a sign pointing to Timber and Vernonia. Follow this road (**Timber Road**) for the next 20 miles as it climbs up and down the foothills to the town of Timber at mile 30.9, crosses Highway 26 at mile 34.1, then follows the Nehalem River toward Vernonia.

44.5 Turn left at a T-intersection with **Highway 47**, then follow Highway 47 through Vernonia, where it becomes **Bridge Street**. (Anderson Park—camping permitted; drinking water available—is located three blocks south of the route as it passes through "downtown" Vernonia. To reach the park, turn right on Adams Avenue at mile 46.6. A day-use park on Rock Creek is located northeast of that same intersection.)

47.7 Follow Highway 47 when it turns left immediately after crossing a bridge over the Nehalem River.

52.0 Turn right, leaving Highway 47, at a sign pointing to Scappoose and St. Helens (**Vernonia-Scappoose Road**).

57.6 Scaponia Recreation Area (camping, picnicking, drinking water). From Scaponia, the road continues to climb, reaching its highest point (1232 feet) at mile 60.0, after which the route begins a 12-mile descent to the Columbia River. At mile 68.5, Bonnie Falls are on the south side of the road.

72.8 Turn right on **Highway 30** and follow it through Scappoose. Although the shoulder of Highway 30 is quite adequate, the road is a busy one, so ride carefully. At two points (unmarked roads at mile 73.7 and mile 76.0) sections of the old highway parallel Highway 30 and can be used instead of the shoulder of the newer road.

76.8 Turn right on **Rocky Point Road** and prepare yourself for several miles of very steep road.

80.1 Turn left on **Skyline Boulevard**. The elevation at this intersection is 1475 feet, the highest of the ride.

84.8 Turn right on **Elliot Road**. A few feet after this intersection, the road begins to drop into the Tualatin Valley.

85.5 Turn right at a T-intersection with **Rock Creek Road**.

89.8 Make a hard right turn onto **Old Cornelius Pass Road**.

91.2 Turn right on **Phillips Road**.

93.5 Turn left at a T-intersection with **Helvetia Road**.

94.5 Bear right (west) onto **West Union Road**.

94.6 West Union School. End of ride.

44 THREE-FERRY FIGURE EIGHT

Starting Point: Wheatland Ferry, south of Dayton near Maude Williamson State Park, or drive west from I-5 exit 263 or 271. Park on either side of the river.

Distance: Total, 147.4 miles: 59.3 first day; 88.1 second day.

Terrain: Moderate; generally level with some hills.

Total Cumulative Elevation Gain: Total, 3150 feet: 1700 first day; 1450 second day.

Recommended Time of Year: Any season except winter and early spring.

Recommended Starting Time: 9:00 A.M.

Allow: 2 days.

Points of Interest
Wheatland Ferry
Canby Ferry
Buena Vista Ferry
Four state parks
Willamette River
  Greenway parks
Numerous city and county parks
Ankeny National Wildlife Refuge

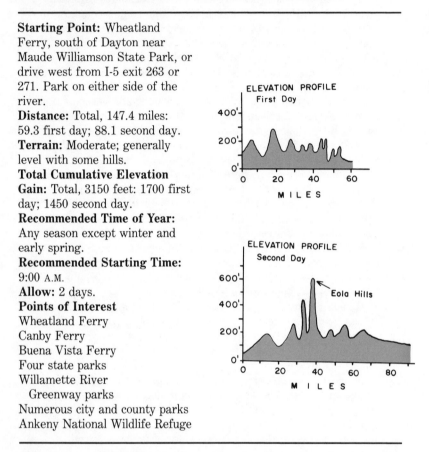

ELEVATION PROFILE
First Day

ELEVATION PROFILE
Second Day

Eola Hills

  Back when the Willamette River had few bridges over it, the only way to cross the river was by ferry. The ferries were small, primitive craft, privately operated by farmers attempting to supplement their income or real estate speculators eager to lure commerce to their riverside communities.

  Of the nearly two dozen ferries that once operated on the Willamette, only three remain. The Wheatland Ferry, north of Salem, made its first crossing in 1844. The Buena Vista Ferry, located midway between Albany and Independence, has been operating since the early 1850s. The youngest of the surviving ferries, at Canby, was started in only 1915.

  This figure-eight loop includes all three of the ferries, with the Buena Vista Ferry at its southern end, the Canby Ferry at its northern end, and the Wheatland Ferry at the crossroads in the center. Although the Buena Vista Ferry does not currently run on weekends, weekend riders can still take this trip by using a bridge a few miles downstream at Independence, which shortens the second day of the ride by 18.4 miles.

Until recently these three ferries were operated without charge by the counties in which they run, but small tolls are now charged motorists (but not bicyclists) by the ferries at Wheatland and Buena Vista, and a toll is being considered at Canby. Because the tolls are subject to change, carry some extra funds just in case.

The route can be started at any point and can be ridden in several different directions, but careful planning is necessary due to the length of the ride, the several ferry crossings, and the presence of only one campground on the route. The itinerary described below is designed to roughly divide the riding between two days and uses Champoeg State Park as the overnight stop. It starts at the center of the figure eight, the Wheatland Ferry, then proceeds north on the west side of the Willamette River. In order to avoid Highway 99W in the Newberg/Dayton area, the route makes a detour through the Chehalem Valley. After crossing the river on the Canby Ferry, the route turns west on its south side (the Willamette flows east here) to Champoeg State Park, for a first-day total of 59.3 miles. On the second day, the route turns south to Wheatland, crosses to the west side of the Willamette, heads south to the Buena Vista Ferry (or, on weekends, the Independence bridge), and then returns on the east bank to Wheatland, for a second-day total of 88.1 miles (69.7 miles if the Independence bridge is used).

The itinerary is also designed to deliver the rider to each ferry during its operating hours. At the time of publication, the operating hours were:

Canby Ferry	10:00 A.M. to 7:00 P.M. seven days a week
Wheatland Ferry	6:00 A.M. to 9:45 P.M. seven days a week
Buena Vista Ferry	7:00 A.M. to 8:50 P.M. Monday through Friday

When planning the ride, check to make sure that the hours shown above are still accurate. Information can be obtained by calling the respective county road departments during normal business hours. The phone numbers are: Canby Ferry, 655-8521; Wheatland Ferry, 588-5036; Buena Vista Ferry, 623-9287. In winter and spring, these numbers should also be used to find out if the ferries have stopped running altogether, since none of the ferries operate during periods of high water. The Buena Vista Ferry may also be closed in late summer if the water level is unusually low. Call ahead to avoid disappointment.

On your second crossing on the Wheatland Ferry, you can leave your overnight gear in your car, which will be parked nearby, although the gear may be safer on your bike.

Despite these logistical problems, this figure-eight loop is well worth the

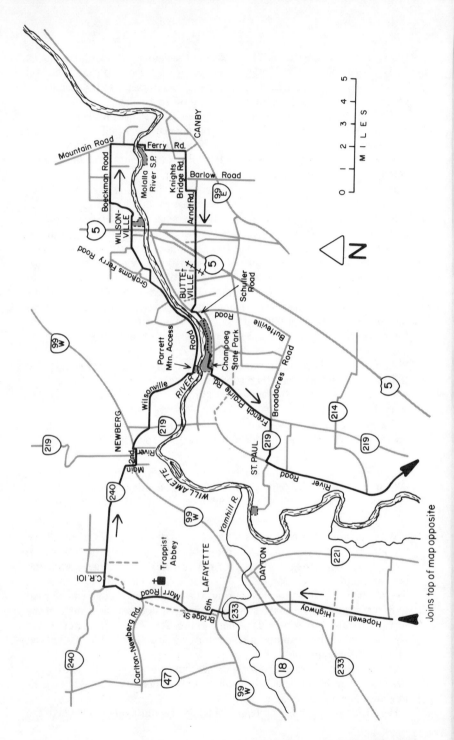

Joins top of map opposite

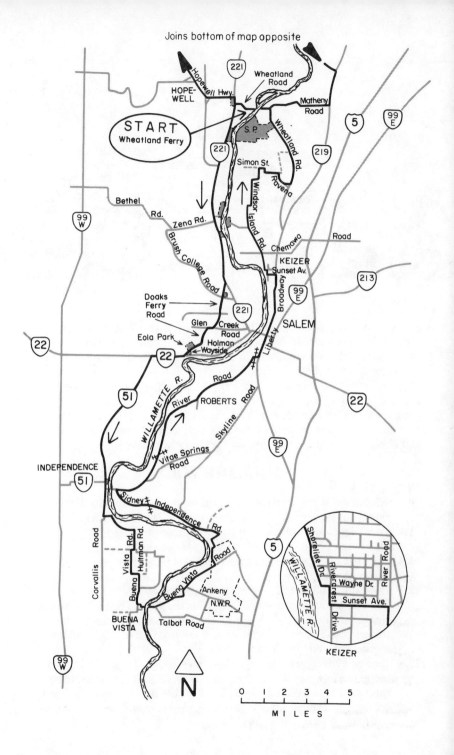

effort. It covers both sides of the river in the heart of its valley, passes through four counties, makes four ferry crossings, visits more than a dozen parks, and, with the exception of a section that passes through the center of Salem, is relatively free of traffic.

Riders preferring shorter, one-day rides can use the mileage log below to ride the 79.4-mile loop between Wheatland and Canby, the 68.0-mile loop between Wheatland and Buena Vista, the 49.6-mile loop between Wheatland and Independence, or even the 19.4-mile loop between Independence and Buena Vista. Just make sure the ferries are running.

MILEAGE LOG

FIRST DAY

0.0 Wheatland Ferry. Park on either side of the ferry crossing, but start riding on the west side by heading west on **Wheatland Road**.

1.1 Turn right on **Highway 221**. The entrance to Maude Williamson State Park is across this intersection (day use only; water available).

1.4 Turn left on an unmarked road (**Hopewell Highway**; sign points to Hopewell and McMinnville).

2.7 Hopewell. Follow the arterial through this very small community. The schoolhouse on the left dates from ca. 1900. The church on the right is an 1880 remodeling of an older structure. At mile 2.8, follow the arterial (Hopewell Highway) as it curves right (north) at an intersection with Webfoot Road.

10.8 Ride straight (north) through this intersection. Hopewell Highway becomes **Highway 233** at this point. At mile 11.3, continue straight through an intersection with Highway 18. At mile 13.3, the road crosses the Yamhill River on a bridge, then passes Terry Park on the left (day use only; no water).

13.6 Lafayette. Highway 233 ends here; continue north on **Madison Street** through an intersection with Highway 99W.

13.8 Turn left on **Sixth Street**. The Yamhill County Historical Society Museum is on the right.

14.0 Turn right (north) on **Bridge Street** and follow it as it becomes **Marr Road** and proceeds through the foothills and farmland north of Lafayette. Our Lady of Guadalupe Trappist Abbey is on the right at mile 16.9. At mile 18.0, bear right, staying on Marr Road.

19.9 T-intersection with **Highway 240**. Turn right. At mile 20.5, continue east on Highway 240 at an intersection with County Road 101. An abandoned 1909 one-room schoolhouse stands on the south side of this intersection.

25.7 Highway 240 turns south and enters Newberg as **Main Street**. At mile 26.0, Main Street crosses the two one-way streets that pass through Newberg as Highway 99W.

26.1 Turn left on **Second Street**.

26.6 T-intersection with **River Street**. Turn left. On the left is the Min-thorn House, boyhood home of Herbert Hoover. Opposite is Hoover Memorial Park (day use only).

26.7 Turn right on **Highway 99W**. A sidewalk is available on the south side of this busy road, or a path through Hoover Park may be used.

26.8 Turn right on **Highway 219**.

28.2 Turn left on **Wilsonville Road** and follow it east for several miles along the Willamette River. At mile 32.6, Parrett Mountain Access, a Willamette Greenway public use area, allows access to the river. At mile 37.7, follow Wilsonville Road as it bears right at an intersection with Grahams Ferry Road. At mile 39.4, a bike lane becomes available on the right as the road enters Wilsonville.

40.4 Wilsonville (store). Continue east on Wilsonville Road. Wilsonville Memorial Park is on the right at mile 40.9 (day use only; water available).

42.6 Turn right (east) at a T-intersection with **Boeckman Road**.

42.7 Although the arterial turns left here, continue straight (east) on Boeckman Road. At mile 43.3, beware of a short, but very steep, hill with rough pavement.

45.4 Turn right (south) at a T-intersection with **Mountain Road**.

46.5 Follow the arterial by turning left, down a hill.

46.7 Canby Ferry Landing. After the ferry crossing, continue south on **Ferry Road**. The Molalla River State Park is to the right, down a short road, at mile 47.2 (day use only; drinking water available).

49.2 Turn right on **Knights Bridge Road** near a small city park. The road crosses the Molalla River at mile 49.9.

51.4 Turn right at a T-intersection with **Arndt Road**. Cross the Pudding River on a bridge at mile 51.8 and follow Arndt Road west for several miles.

57.0 Butteville (store). Turn left on **Butteville Road**. A bike lane begins on the right one block later.

57.2 Turn right on **Schuller Road**, following the bike lane.

57.6 Follow the bike path when it bears left, leaving Schuller Road. The bike path proceeds west through the woods, along the Willamette, to Champoeg State Park.

59.3 T-intersection with a paved road in Champoeg State Park. On the right is a bridge over Champoeg Creek. Turn left to the overnight camp. The park has several interesting features, including an excellent visitors center and several miles of bike paths.

SECOND DAY

0.0 Leave Champoeg State Park overnight camp and follow the signs to the park entrance.

1.0 Park entrance. Turn right on **Champoeg Road**. At mile 1.1, the Robert Newell House museum is on the right.

1.2 T-intersection with **French Prairie Road** (Champoeg Road). Turn left (south).

4.7 Turn right on **Highway 219**, following the signs to St. Paul.

6.6 St. Paul (store). Turn left (south) on **Main Street**, which soon becomes **River Road**.

14.7 Turn right at a T-intersection with **Highway 219**.

16.4 Turn right on **Matheny Road**.

19.6 Turn right, following Matheny Road.

20.1 Wheatland Ferry. After crossing the river, continue west on **Wheatland Road**.

21.2 Turn left at an intersection with **Highway 221**. Maude Williamson State Park (day use only; water available) is directly west of this intersection. At mile 23.5, Spring Valley Access, a Willamette Greenway park, allows access to the river. Another access area can be reached by turning left on Lincoln Road at mile 26.7 (store), and a third is located at mile 27.7.

29.9 Turn right on **Doaks Ferry Road**. At mile 30.4, Brush College Park is on the left (day use only; drinking water available).

31.9 Bear right at an intersection with **Glen Creek Road**.

32.1 Turn left (south), following **Doaks Ferry Road**. Eola Park (day use only; water available) is on the right at mile 33.7.

34.3 T-intersection with **Highway 22**. Turn right and proceed west using the bike path on the north side of this busy highway. Holman Wayside (day use only; water available) is northeast of this intersection.

35.7 Turn left on **Highway 51** and follow it to Independence, where it becomes **Main Street**.

42.2 Independence (store). Polk Marine Park (day use only; water available) is on the left at the foot of B Street.

42.7 The Independence bridge is on the left. (If the Buena Vista Ferry is not running—the ferry is closed on weekends—or if you prefer to shorten the ride by 18.4 miles, turn left here. At the east end of the 0.5-mile bridge, you will rejoin the route at mile 61.6, below.) Continue south on Main Street, which soon becomes **Corvallis Road**.

43.7 Turn left on **Buena Vista Road** (Hartman Road).

46.3 Turn right on Buena Vista Road (Davidson Road). Wigrich Road goes straight here.

46.5 Turn left (south) on Buena Vista Road. Davidson Road goes straight (west) from this intersection.

47.9 Follow Buena Vista Road when it turns right (south) at an intersection with Hultman Road.

49.5 Buena Vista. Turn left on **Sequoia Street** and follow it as it turns right and becomes **Riverview Street** at mile 49.6.

49.7 Turn left (east) on Willamette Ferry Street, following the signs to the ferry landing. Buena Vista Park (day use only) is one block south of an intersection at mile 49.8.

49.9 Buena Vista Ferry. After crossing the river, ride east on **Buena Vista Road**. Bear left at an intersection with Talbot Road at mile 50.2.

53.9 Turn left on **Sidney-Independence Road** (County Road 852) immediately after crossing a small bridge over an irrigation ditch. This intersection is located within the Ankeny National Wildlife Refuge. During the winter, watch for huge flocks of dusky Canada geese. Follow this road through several 90-degree turns as it works its way north.

61.5 Just before passing under the east approach to the Independence bridge, turn right (east).

61.6 Turn right on **River Road** and follow it east and north to Salem. Halls Ferry Access, a Willamette Greenway day use area, is on the left at mile 65.6.

68.1 Roberts (store). Follow River Road as it bears left. At mile 70.6, the entrance to Minto-Brown Island Park (day use only) is on the left. A bike path begins on the east side of River Road at this point. At mile 71.6, River Road curves right (east) and becomes **Owens Street**.

71.9 Turn left at a T-intersection with **Liberty Street** and follow it north through downtown Salem. Ride carefully on this busy one-way street. Although sidewalks are available on both sides, not all of the curbs are cut for bikes, and bikes are not allowed on sidewalks downtown between Ferry Street (mile 72.5) and Union Street (mile 73.0).

73.1 Bear right on Liberty Street (now Highway 219), which crosses a bridge over Mill Creek and becomes a two-way street.

73.3 Turn left on **Broadway Street** (Highway 219) and follow it north.

75.1 Continue north when Broadway joins **River Road** (Highway 219). A new bike path/sidewalk on the west side of the road, which was under construction when this book went to press, will probably be the safest route.

75.9 Keizer. Turn left on **Sunset Avenue**.

76.3 Turn right (north) on **Rivercrest Drive**. River Edge Park (day use only; no drinking water) is just west of this intersection.

76.5 Turn left on **Wayne Drive**, which curves north and becomes **Shoreline Drive**. At mile 77.3, Shoreline Drive crosses Chemawa Road and becomes **Windsor Island Road**. (At mile 78.7, a one-mile detour west on Naples Street leads to Spongs Landing Park—day use only; drinking water available.)

81.9 Turn right at a T-intersection with **Simon Street** and follow it as it becomes **9th Avenue** and then **Salmon Street**.

82.9 Turn right on **Ravena Drive**.

83.8 Bear left when the road forks.

84.0 Turn left on **Wheatland Road**. Willamette Mission State Park is on the left at mile 86.8 (day use only; water available).

87.7 Turn left (west) on **Matheny Road**.

88.1 Wheatland Ferry landing. End of ride.

INDICES

Alphabetical Index

Trip Junctions

In order to help readers connect two or more of the described routes, listed below are towns, parks, or other sites where the routes cross paths. In a few cases, the routes do not actually cross, but pass within a mile or two.

Trip Junctions (Continued)

Junction	Trip Number	Junction	Trip Number
Farmington	6, 7, 8	Mount Angel	25, 26
Fern Ridge Lake	39, 40	Needy	18, 26
Feyrer Park	17, 18	Newberg	13, 19, 44
Forest Grove	8, 10, 43	Perrydale	22, 23, 29
Gervais	24, 25	Portland Womens Forum State	
Harrisburg	35, 37, 38, 39	Park	1, 2
Hillsboro	8, 43	St. Louis	24, 25
Hillside	10, 43	St. Paul	24, 25
Holman Wayside	29, 44	Scholls	6, 7, 13, 19
Hopewell	21, 22, 44	Sherwood	7, 13
Independence	29, 30, 44	Skyline Boulevard	5, 43
Jefferson	28, 31	Springdale	1, 3
Lafayette	20, 40	Springwater	15, 17
Lancaster	37, 38, 39	Suver	30, 36
Larwood	31, 32	Troutdale	1, 3
Lebanon	32, 34	Verboort	8, 43
Lewis and Clark State Park	1, 3	West Union	5, 9, 43
Maude Williamson State		Wheatland Ferry	21, 22, 25, 44
Park	21, 22, 44	Whiskey Hill	18, 26
Meadowbrook	17, 18	Wilsonville	13, 44
Molalla River State Park	18	Yamhill	19, 20

Mileage Index

Miles	Trip Name	Number	Miles	Trip Name	Number
11.0	Hagg Lake	11	30.0	Lafayette	20
12.4	Sauvie Island	4	30.2	Larch Mountain	2
19.4	Petes Mountain	14	31.5	Chehalem Mountains	
19.7	Farmington–Scholls			(short loop)	19
	Loop	6	32.1	Upper Yamhill Valley	23
22.3	Mountaindale	9	32.8	Fern Ridge	40
24.2	Lolo Pass	12	32.8	South French Prairie	25
25.6	Gales Creek	10	33.2	Skyline Boulevard	5
28.5	Luckiamute Loops (east		33.9	North Santiam (east	
	loop)	30		loop)	28
28.7	Luckiamute Loops (west		34.3	South Santiam (short	
	loop)	30		loop)	32
29.6	Molalla–Pudding (Pudding		34.4	Lower Tualatin Valley	7
	River loop)	18	34.5	North Santiam (west	
				loop)	28

Mileage Index (Continued)